Educating
for Eternity

Educating for Eternity

A Seventh-day Adventist
Philosophy of Education

George R. Knight

Andrews
University Press

Berrien Springs, Michigan

Andrews University Press
Sutherland House
8360 W. Campus Circle Dr.
Berrien Springs, MI 49104–1700
Telephone: 269–471–6134; Fax: 269–471–6224
Email: aupo@andrews.edu
Website: http://universitypress.andrews.edu

ISBN (paperback) 978-1-940980-12-6
ISBN (e-book) 978-1-940980-13-3

Printed in the United States of America
20 19 18 17 16   2 3 4 5 6

Unless otherwise indicated, Scripture quotations are taken from the Revised Standard Version of the Bible, copyright © 1946, 1952, and 1971 by the Division of Christian Education of the National Council of the Churches of Christ in the United States of America. Used by permission. All rights reserved. Scripture quotations marked KJV are taken from the authorized King James Version.

Library of Congress Cataloging-in-Publication Data

Names: Knight, George R., author.
Title: Educating for eternity : a Seventh-day Adventist philosophy of
  education / George R. Knight.
Description: Berrien Springs, MI : Andrews University Press, [2016] |
  Includes bibliographical references and index.
Identifiers: LCCN 2016021742 (print) | LCCN 2016035156 (ebook) | ISBN
  9781940980126 (pbk. : alk. paper) | ISBN 9781940980133 (e-book) | ISBN
  9781940980133 ()
Subjects: LCSH: Seventh-day Adventists--Education.
Classification: LCC LC586.S48 K55 2016 (print) | LCC LC586.S48 (ebook) | DDC
  371.071--dc23
LC record available at https://lccn.loc.gov/2016021742

Typeset: 10.5/14 Minion Pro

Dedicated to
Brenda and Rodney Payne II,
beloved children with whom I share the journey
toward God's eternal kingdom

"An education that fails to consider the fundamental questions of human existence—the questions about the meaning of life and the nature of truth, goodness, beauty, and justice, with which philosophy is concerned—is a very inadequate type of education."

—Harold Titus

"Our ideas of education take too narrow and too low a range. There is need of a broader scope, a higher aim. True education means more than the pursual of a certain course of study. It means more than a preparation for the life that now is. It has to do with the whole being, and with the whole period of existence possible to man. It is the harmonious development of the physical, the mental, and the spiritual powers. It prepares the student for the joy of service in this world and for the higher joy of wider service in the world to come."

—Ellen G. White

"Through sin the divine likeness was marred, and well-nigh obliterated. Man's physical powers were weakened, his mental capacity was lessened, his spiritual vision dimmed. He had become subject to death. Yet the race was not left without hope. By infinite love and mercy the plan of salvation had been devised, and a life of probation was granted. To restore in man the image of his Maker, to bring him back to the perfection in which he was created, to promote the development of body, mind, and soul, that the divine purpose in his creation might be realized—this was to be the work of redemption. This is the object of education, the great object of life."

—Ellen G. White

"And this is eternal life, that they know thee the only true God, and Jesus Christ whom thou hast sent."

—Jesus

CONTENTS ●

LIST OF FIGURES

A WORD TO THE READER

If you don't know where you are going, you will never get there. That seemingly obvious fact undergirds this book. Destinations in both life and in educational institutions are all-important. After all, why spend endless energy and money on the trip if you are heading in the wrong direction?

But how does one decide on direction? The answer to that question drives us to the most basic questions that people can ask about the meaning and purpose of life—questions related to the nature of ultimate reality, the means of arriving at truth, and the essential values. These are the questions that philosophy seeks to answer. And the different answers to them provide the starting point for all philosophies of education.

It goes without saying that varying philosophies of education lead to radically different approaches to education in terms of what a system of schools hopes to achieve, the role its teachers should perform, the curricular emphasis, the best teaching strategies, and the social implications of the school.

Educating for Eternity: A Seventh-day Adventist Philosophy of Education examines the basic philosophic issues from a biblical/ Christian/Adventist perspective and sets forth the educational implications of such a philosophy. Surprisingly enough, given the fact that Adventism sponsors nearly 8,000 schools, this is the first book-length treatment of the philosophy of Adventist education—a topic that is significantly different from a general Christian perspective on the topic.

The purpose of this slim volume is not to treat the subject comprehensively, but to set forth its general shape and content. It is written with teachers, educational administrators, school board members, parents, pastors, and teachers in mind. The material in this book was originally developed for the denomination's General Conference Department of Education's continuing education program. It was also published in *The Journal of Adventist Education* under the title of "Redemptive Education."

Given its brevity, *Educating for Eternity* does not attempt to cover the full range of topics important to a broad understanding of the philosophy of education. I have undertaken that task in my *Philosophy and Education: An Introduction in Christian Perspective* (4th ed., 2006). That volume covers in much greater depth basic concepts related to both philosophy and education; explores and critiques from a Christian perspective the relationship of traditional, modern, and postmodern philosophies to the world of education; and indicates how the more formal approaches of the philosophic "schools" have undergirded the various educational theories that have been developed over the past century. *Philosophy and Education* also has chapters on both the relationship of analytic philosophy to education and the role of Christian teachers in public schools.

With those facts in mind, *Educating for Eternity*, even though it provides a helpful stand-alone treatment of the topic of the philosophy of education, for best results needs to be read within the context of the broader treatment provided by *Philosophy and Education*. The two books are complementary even though both of them adequately survey their topics of focus.

Another of my books that helps fill out the picture is *Myths in Adventism: An Interpretive Study of Ellen White, Education, and Related Issues* (1985, 2009). This volume is especially helpful in exploring in more depth specific issues related to the philosophy of Adventist education. That same topic from a historical perspective is the theme of my edited volume of essays that was published under the title of *Early Adventist Educators* in 1983. It is my hope to develop someday an integrated book on the historical development of Adventist educational thought against the backdrop of the history of Adventist education.

Meanwhile, it is my prayer that *Educating for Eternity* will prove an insightful introduction to the philosophy of Adventist education.

I would like to express appreciation to Beverly Rumble for her persistence in encouraging the project; to my wife, Bonnie, for typing the book manuscript; and to Ronald Knott and Deborah Everhart of Andrews University Press for shepherding it through the publication process.

George R. Knight
Rogue River, Oregon

PART I

Philosophic Foundations

Philosophic Issues and Their Relevance for Education

W hy study philosophy of education? After all, time is short, and there are so many practical things to learn. Why waste precious hours on something so esoteric and useless?

Those are good questions that remind me of the multitude of laws that populate our world. The world, as we all know, is full of laws—not only in the physical realm, but also in the social. I have been collecting these enlightening laws for some years:

- *Schmidt's Law:* "If you mess with a thing long enough, it will break."
- *Weiler's Law:* "Nothing is impossible for the man who doesn't have to do it himself."
- *Jones's Law:* "The person who can smile when things go wrong has thought of someone to blame it on."
- *Boob's Law:* "You always find something in the last place you look for it."

Having been enlightened by such wisdom, I eventually decided to try my hand at developing some cryptic and esoteric sagacity of my own. The result: *Knight's Law* with two corollaries. Put simply, *Knight's Law* reads, "It is impossible to arrive at your destination unless you know where you are going." Corollary Number 1: "A school that does not come close to attaining its goals will eventually lose its support." Corollary Number 2: "We think only when it hurts."

Those bits of "wisdom" were created in my days as a young professor of educational philosophy, when I concluded, as I still believe, that a sound philosophy of education is the most useful and practical item in an educator's repertoire. That is true in part because philosophy at its best deals with the most basic issues of life—such as the nature of reality, truth, and value. Closely related to philosophy is the concept of worldview, which "roughly speaking, . . . refers to a person's interpretation of reality and a basic view of life."[1]

WHY STUDY PHILOSOPHY OF EDUCATION?

People's beliefs about the philosophic issues of reality, truth, and value will determine everything they do in both their personal and professional lives. Without a distinctive philosophic position on those three categories, a person or group cannot make decisions, form a curriculum, or evaluate institutional or individual progress. With a consciously chosen philosophy, however, a person or group can set goals to be achieved and select courses of action to reach those goals.

Of course, a human being can chose to merely wander aimlessly through life and a professional teaching career. Or he or she can operate on the basis of someone else's decision making. The first of those options, if taken seriously, suggests a philosophic belief that life itself is aimless and without clearly defined purposes, while the second may cause a person to act on a well-thought-out philosophy of education but one that might have the disconcerting result of leading in the wrong direction.

I would like to suggest that a consciously thought-out philosophy of education is not only an educator's most practical acquisition, but also his or her most important one. Ellen White (1827–1915), Seventh-day Adventism's prophetic thought leader, held the same viewpoint. "By a misconception of the true nature and object of education," she wrote, "many have been led into serious and even fatal errors [*eternally* fatal in the overall context of her writings].

Such a mistake is made when the regulation of the heart or the establishment of principles is neglected in the effort to secure intellectual culture, or when eternal interests are overlooked in the eager desire for temporal advantage."[2]

Again, she wrote, "the necessity of establishing Christian schools is urged upon me very strongly. In the schools of today many things are taught that are a hindrance rather than a blessing. Schools are needed where the word of God is made the basis of education. Satan is the great enemy of God, and it is his constant aim to lead souls away from their allegiance to the King of heaven. He would have minds so trained that men and women will exert their influence on the side of error and moral corruption, instead of using their talents in the service of God. His object is effectually gained, when by perverting their ideas of education, he succeeds in enlisting parents and teachers on his side; for a wrong education often starts the mind on the road to infidelity."[3]

Such thoughts down through history have led various Christian denominations, including Seventh-day Adventists, to go to great expense and effort to establish their own schools. Providing greater urgency has been the Adventists' conviction that each of the church's children (as well as the church itself) is caught in the midst of a great struggle between good and evil. Therefore, the church moved proactively to establish an educational system based on not only a general Christian understanding of reality, truth, and value, but one that also reflects distinctively Adventist understandings.

Coming to grips with the undergirding ideas that have led to the establishment and operation of Seventh-day Adventist schools is the realm of an Adventist philosophy of education. Of course, grappling with basic ideas is only part of the task. Other aspects include developing practices in harmony with those foundational understandings and implementing them in the life of the school. The first two of those goals fit under the rubric of educational philosophy. The practical aspect is the educator's responsibility to implement after consciously thinking through both his or her core beliefs and also how those beliefs can and should impact daily life and professional practice.

Before moving to a discussion of the basic issues of philosophy, it is important to point out that a philosophy of education is much broader than a philosophy of schooling. Schools are only one aspect of any social group's educational system. The family, media, peer group, and church also share the responsibility for educating the next generation, with the family holding the dominant role. That fact must be recognized even though this book will use categories that are most often linked with schooling. But the insights being shared are just as important to educators in the church and family as they are to teachers in the school. The best overall educational experience, of course, takes place when parents, teachers, and church leaders all share the same concerns and provide a learning environment in which each student experiences a unified education rather than a schizophrenic one in which the significant educators espouse different views. With that in mind, it is no accident that Seventh-day Adventists have gone to the effort and expense of establishing a system that currently has almost 8,000 schools.

Different systems of education have varying goals, and those goals are based on differing philosophies of education. With that thought in mind, we now turn to an examination of the issues basic to philosophy, followed by a look at the Christian/Adventist understanding of those issues. Lastly, we will examine the educational practices that flow out of those understandings.

Philosophy deals with the most basic issues faced by human beings. The content of philosophy is better seen as asking questions rather than providing answers. It can even be said that *philosophy is the study of questions*. Van Cleve Morris has noted that the crux of the matter is asking the "right" questions. By "right" he meant questions that are meaningful and relevant—the kind of questions people really want answered and that will make a difference in how they live and work.[4]

Philosophical content has been organized around three fundamental categories:

1. *Metaphysics*—the study of questions concerning the nature of reality;

2. *Epistemology*—the study of the nature of truth and knowledge and how these are attained and evaluated; and

3. *Axiology*—the study of the question of value.

Without a distinctive philosophy of reality, truth, and value, a person or group cannot make intelligent decisions either for their individual lives or for developing an educational system. The questions addressed by philosophy are so basic that there is no escaping them. As a result, all of us, whether we consciously understand our philosophic positions or not, conduct our personal lives and our corporate existence on the basis of answers to the basic questions of life. There is no decision making that is unrelated to the issues of reality, truth, and value. To put it succinctly: *Philosophy drives decision making.* For that reason alone, the study of the foundational questions of philosophy is important. After all, it is better to function with understanding than to wander through life in ignorance of the factors that shape our choices.

With the importance of understanding the basic issues in mind, in the next few pages we will briefly describe the three main philosophic categories and then move on to an Adventist perspective on each of them.

METAPHYSICS

One of the two most basic philosophic categories is metaphysics. That rather threatening-sounding word actually comes from two Greek words meaning "beyond physics." As such, metaphysics is the branch of philosophy that deals with the nature of reality. "What is ultimately real?" is the basic question asked in the study of metaphysics.

At first glance, the answer to that query seems rather obvious. After all, most people seem to be quite certain about the "reality" of their world. If you ask them, they will probably tell you to open your eyes and look at the clock on the wall, to listen to the sound of a passing train, or to bend down to touch the floor beneath your feet. These things are, they claim, what is ultimately real.

But are they? Their answers are located on the plane of physics rather than metaphysics. There are surely more foundational questions. For example, where did the material for floors, the power that runs trains, and the regularity of time ultimately originate? It makes no difference if your answer is related to design, accident, or mystery, because once you have begun to deal with the deeper questions, you have moved beyond physics to the realm of metaphysics.

We can gain a glimpse into the realm of metaphysics by examining a list of major questions concerning the nature of reality. The queries of the metaphysician are amongst the most general questions that can be asked. It is important to realize, however, that people need the answers to these questions before they can find satisfactory answers to their more specific questions. Yet complete verification of any particular answer to these questions is beyond the realm of human demonstration or proof. But that does not make the discussion of these issues irrelevant or a mere exercise in mental gymnastics since people, whether they consciously understand it or not, base their daily activities and long-range goals upon a set of metaphysical beliefs. Even people seeking answers to more specific questions—physicists or biologists or historians, for example—cannot ignore metaphysical questions. Thus, undergirding science is the philosophy of science, and foundational to historical understanding is the philosophy of history. It is the philosophy of science and history that provides the theoretical framework for understanding and interpreting the meaning of the facts in each field.

Metaphysical questions may be divided into four subsets. First, the *cosmological aspect*. Cosmology consists in the study of theories about the origin, nature, and development of the universe as an orderly system. Questions such as these populate the realm of cosmology: "How did the universe originate and develop? Did it come about by accident or design? Does its existence have any purpose?"

A second metaphysical aspect is the *theological*. Theology is that part of religious theory that deals with conceptions of and about God. "Is there a God? If so, is there one or more than one? What are the attributes of God? If God is both all good and all powerful, why does evil exist? If God exists, what is His relationship to human beings and the 'real' world of everyday life?"

People answer such questions in a variety of ways. *Atheists* claim that there is no God, while *pantheists* posit that God and the universe are identical—all is God and God is all. *Deists* view God as the maker of nature and moral laws, but assert that He exists apart from, and is not particularly interested in, the daily events of human lives or the physical universe. On the other hand, *theists* believe in a personal Creator God who has a deep and ongoing interest in His creation. *Polytheism* disagrees with *monotheism* in regard to the number of gods, with polytheists holding that deity should be thought of as plural and monotheists insisting that there is one God.[5]

A third subset of metaphysics is the *anthropological*. Anthropology deals with the study of human beings and asks questions like the following: "What is the relation between mind and body? Is mind more fundamental than body, with body depending on mind, or vice versa?" "What is humanity's moral status? Are people born good, evil, or morally neutral?" "To what extent are individuals free? Do they have free will, or are their thoughts and actions determined by their environment, inheritance, or a divine Being?" "Does each person have a soul? If so, what is it?" People have obviously adopted different positions on these questions, and those positions influence their political, social, religious, and educational ideals and practices.

The fourth aspect of metaphysics is the *ontological*. Ontology is the study of the nature of existence, or what it means for anything to exist. Several questions are central to ontology: "Is basic reality found in matter or physical energy (the world we can sense), or is it found in spirit or spiritual energy? Is it composed of one element (e.g., matter or spirit), or two (e.g., matter and spirit), or many?" "Is reality orderly and lawful in itself, or is it merely orderable by the human mind? Is it fixed and stable, or is change its central feature? Is this reality friendly, unfriendly, or neutral toward humanity?"

Even a cursory study of either historical or contemporary societies will reveal the impact of the cosmological, theological, anthropological, and ontological aspects of metaphysics upon their social, political, economic, and scientific beliefs and practices. People everywhere embrace answers to these questions and then live their daily lives in keeping with those assumptions. There is no escape from metaphysical decisions—unless one chooses to vegetate—and even that choice would be a metaphysical decision about the nature and function of humanity. Education, like other human activities, cannot operate outside the realm of metaphysics. Metaphysics, or the issue of ultimate reality, is central to any concept of education, because it is important for the educational program of the school (or family or church) to be based upon fact and reality rather than fancy, illusion, error, or imagination. Varying metaphysical beliefs lead to differing educational approaches and even separate systems of education.

Why do Adventists and other Christians spend millions of dollars each year on private systems of education when free public systems are widely available? Because of their metaphysical beliefs regarding the nature of ultimate reality, the existence of God, the role of God in human affairs, and the nature and role of human beings as God's children. At their deepest levels, men and women are motivated by metaphysical beliefs. History demonstrates that people are willing to die for those convictions, and that they desire to create educational environments in which their most basic beliefs will be taught to their children.

The anthropological aspect of metaphysics is especially important for educators of all persuasions. After all, they are dealing with malleable human beings at one of the most impressionable stages of their lives. Views about the nature and potential of students form the foundation of every educational process. The very purpose of education in all philosophies is closely tied to these views. Thus, anthropological considerations lie extremely close to the aims of education. Philosopher D. Elton Trueblood put it nicely when he asserted that "until we are clear on what man is, we shall not be clear about much else."[6]

It makes a great deal of difference whether a student is viewed as Desmond Morris's "naked ape"[7] or as a child of God. Likewise, it is important to know whether children are innately evil, essentially good, or good but radically twisted by the effects of sin. Variations in anthropological positions will produce significantly different approaches to the educational process. Other examples of the impact of metaphysics upon education will become evident further on in our study.

EPISTEMOLOGY

Closely related to metaphysics is the issue of epistemology. Epistemology seeks to answer such basic questions as "What is true?" and "How do we know?" The study of epistemology deals with issues related to the dependability of knowledge and the validity of the sources through which we gain information. Accordingly, epistemology stands—with metaphysics—at the very center of the educative process. Because both educational systems as a whole and teachers in those systems deal in knowledge, they are engaged in an epistemological undertaking.

Epistemology seeks answers to a number of fundamental issues. One is whether reality can even be known. *Skepticism* in its narrow sense is the position claiming that people cannot acquire reliable knowledge and that any search for truth is in vain. That thought was well expressed by Gorgias (c. 483–376 B.C.), the Greek Sophist who asserted that nothing exists, and that if it did, we could not know it. A full-blown skepticism would make intelligent action impossible. A term closely related to skepticism is *agnosticism*. Agnosticism is a profession of ignorance concerning the existence or nonexistence of God.

Most people claim that reality can be known. However, once they have taken that position, they must decide through what sources reality may be known, and they must have some concept of how to judge the validity of their knowledge.

A second issue foundational to epistemology is whether all truth is relative, or whether some truths are absolute. Is all truth subject to change? Is it possible that what is true today may be false tomorrow? If the answer is yes to the previous questions, such truths are relative. If, however, there is Absolute Truth, such Truth is eternally and universally true irrespective of time or place. If Absolute Truth exists in the universe, then educators would certainly want to discover it and make it the core of the school curriculum. Closely related to the issue of the relativity and absoluteness of truth are the questions of whether knowledge is subjective or objective, and whether there is truth that is independent of human experience.

A major aspect of epistemology relates to the sources of human knowledge. If one accepts the fact that there is truth and even Truth in the universe, how can human beings comprehend such truths? How do they become human knowledge?

Central to most people's answer to that question is *empiricism* (knowledge obtained through the senses). Empirical knowledge appears to be built into the very nature of human experience. Thus, when individuals walk out of doors on a spring day and see the beauty of the landscape, hear the song of a bird, feel the warm rays of the sun, and smell the fragrance of the blossoms, they know that it is spring. Sensory knowing for humans is immediate and universal, and in many ways forms the basis of much of human knowledge.

The existence of sensory data cannot be denied. Most people accept it uncritically as representing "reality." The danger of naively embracing this approach is that data obtained from the human senses have been demonstrated at times to be both incomplete and undependable. (For example, most people have been confronted with the contradiction of seeing a stick that looks bent when partially submerged in water but appears to be straight when examined in the air.) Fatigue, frustration, and illness also distort and limit sensory perception. In addition, there are sound and light waves that are inaudible and invisible to unaided human perception.

Humans have invented scientific instruments to extend the range of their senses, but it is impossible to ascertain the exact dependability of these instruments since no one knows the total effect of the human mind in recording, interpreting, and distorting sensual perception. Confidence in these instruments is built upon speculative metaphysical theories whose validity has been reinforced by experimentation in which predictions have been verified through the use of a theoretical construct or hypothesis.

In summary, sensory knowledge is built upon assumptions that must be accepted by faith in the dependability of human sensory mechanisms. The advantage of empirical knowledge is that many sensory experiences and experiments are open to both replication and public examination.

A second influential source of knowledge throughout the span of human history has been *revelation*. Revealed knowledge has been of prime importance in the field of religion. It differs from all other sources of knowledge because it presupposes a transcendent supernatural reality that breaks into the natural order. Christians believe that such revelation is God's communication concerning the divine will.

Believers in supernatural revelation hold that this form of knowledge has the distinct advantage of being an omniscient source of information that is not available through other epistemological methods. The truth revealed through this source is believed by Christians to be absolute and uncontaminated. On the other hand, it is generally realized that distortion of revealed truth can occur in the process of human interpretation. Some people assert that a major disadvantage of revealed knowledge is that it must be accepted by faith and cannot be proved or disproved empirically.

A third source of human knowledge is *authority*. Authoritative knowledge is accepted as true because it comes from experts or has been sanctified over time as tradition. In the classroom, the most common source of information is some authority, such as a textbook, teacher, or reference work.

Accepting authority as a source of knowledge has its advantages as well as its dangers. Civilization would certainly stagnate if people refused to accept any statement unless they personally verified it through direct, firsthand experience. On the other hand, if authoritative knowledge is built upon a foundation of incorrect assumptions, then such knowledge will surely be distorted.

A fourth source of human knowledge is *reason*. The view that reasoning, thought, or logic is the central factor in knowledge is known as *rationalism*. The rationalist, in emphasizing humanity's power of thought and the mind's contributions to knowledge, is likely to claim that the senses alone cannot provide universal, valid judgments that are consistent with one another. From this perspective, the sensations and experiences humans obtain through their senses are the raw material of knowledge. These sensations must be organized by the mind into a meaningful system before they become knowledge.

Rationalism in a less extreme form claims that people have the power to know with certainty various truths about the universe that the senses alone cannot give. In its more extreme form, rationalism claims that humans are capable of arriving at irrefutable knowledge independently of sensory experience.

Formal logic is a tool used by rationalists. Systems of logic have the advantage of possessing internal consistency, but they risk being disconnected from the external world. Systems of thought based upon logic are only as valid as the premises upon which they are built.

A fifth source of knowledge is *intuition*—the direct apprehension of knowledge that is not derived from conscious reasoning or immediate sense perception. In the literature dealing with intuition, one often finds such expressions as "immediate feeling of certainty." Intuition occurs beneath the threshold of consciousness and is often experienced as a sudden flash of insight. Intuition has been claimed under varying circumstances as a source of both religious and secular knowledge. Certainly many scientific breakthroughs have been initiated by intuitive hunches that were confirmed by experimentation.

The weakness or danger of intuition is that it does not appear to be a reliable method of obtaining knowledge when used alone. It goes astray very easily and may lead to absurd claims unless it is controlled by or checked against other methods of knowing. Intuitive knowledge, however, has the distinct advantage of being able to bypass the limitations of human experience.

What might be thought of as a sixth avenue to knowledge has been set forth by postmodern theorists. In a vigorous reaction to modernism with its heavy reliance on empirical knowledge and reason, this perspective rejects objective truth and overarching metanarratives or worldviews. Rather than being a reflection of reality, knowledge is viewed as a social construction based on the subjective use of language.

While the social construction approach to knowledge has been helpful in highlighting the subjective aspect of human knowing (i.e., nobody is unbiased), a major weakness is that taking that insight to its extreme undermines any possible coherent and responsible foundation for science, let alone the more nebulous realms of beauty and goodness.

At this juncture, it should be noted that no one source of information is capable of supplying people with all knowledge. The various sources should be seen as complementary rather than antagonistic. It is true, however, that most people choose one source as being more basic than, or preferable to, the others. That most basic source is then used as a benchmark for testing other sources of knowledge. For example, from the perspective of the modernistic worldview knowledge obtained empirically is generally seen as the most basic and reliable type. Most people denigrate any purported knowledge that does not agree with scientific theory. By way of contrast, biblical Christianity sees revelation as providing the basic framework against which other sources of knowledge must be tested.

Epistemology has a direct impact upon education on a moment-by-moment basis. For example, assumptions about the importance of various sources of knowledge will certainly be reflected in curricular emphases and teaching methodologies. Because Christian teachers believe in revelation as a source of valid knowledge, they will undoubtedly choose a curriculum and a role for the Bible in that curriculum that differs substantially from the curricular choices of nonbelievers. In fact, the philosophic worldview of their faith will shape the presentation of every topic they teach. That, of course, is true for teachers from every philosophic persuasion and thus constitutes an important argument for educating Adventist youth in Adventist schools.

THE METAPHYSICAL-EPISTEMOLOGICAL DILEMMA

The careful reader has probably realized by now that humanity, so to speak, is suspended in midair both metaphysically and epistemologically. Our problem: It is impossible to make statements about reality without first adopting a theory for arriving at truth. On the other hand, a theory of truth cannot be developed without first having a concept of reality. We are caught in a web of circularity.

Through the study of basic questions people are forced to recognize their smallness and helplessness in the universe. They realize that nothing can be known for certain in the sense of final and ultimate proof that is open and acceptable to all people, not even in the natural sciences. Trueblood affirmed that point when he wrote that "it is now widely recognized that absolute proof is something which the human being does not and cannot have. This follows necessarily from the twin fact that deductive reasoning cannot have certainty about its premises and that inductive reasoning cannot have certainty about its conclusions. The notion that, in natural science, we have both certainty and absolute proof is simply one of the superstitions of our age."[8] Every person—the skeptic and the agnostic, the scientist and the businessperson, the Hindu and the Christian—lives by a faith. The acceptance of a particular metaphysical and epistemological position is a faith-choice made by each person, and entails a commitment to a way of life.

The circular nature of the reality-truth dilemma is certainly a distressing aspect of philosophical thought; but since it exists, human beings are obligated to make themselves aware of its implications. Of course, this dilemma comes as no surprise to mature scientists who have come to grips with the limitations of their discipline and the philosophy upon which it is built. Neither does it pose a threat to believers in certain religious persuasions who have traditionally viewed their basic beliefs in terms of personal choice, faith, and commitment. The whole problem, however, does come as a source of shock and distress to the average secular individual.

The result of the metaphysical-epistemological dilemma is that all persons live by faith in the basic beliefs they have chosen. The challenge is not in having to make a choice, but making the most adequate choice that takes into consideration the full range of realities and knowledges human beings possess. In chapter 2 we will begin to explore a Christian/Adventist approach to the major philosophic issues. But we first need to explore the third great philosophic issue—*axiology,* or the question of values.

AXIOLOGY

Axiology is the branch of philosophy that seeks to answer the question, "What is of value?" All rational individual and social life is based upon a system of values. Value systems are not universally agreed upon, and different positions on the questions of metaphysics and epistemology produce different value systems because axiological systems are built upon conceptions of reality and truth.

The question of values deals with notions of what a person or a society regards as good or preferable. Axiology, like metaphysics and epistemology, stands at the very foundation of the educational process. A major aspect of education is the development of values. And in that context, the classroom is an axiological theater in which teachers cannot hide their moral selves. By their actions, teachers constantly instruct groups of highly impressionable young people who assimilate and imitate their teachers' value structures to a significant extent.

Axiology has two main branches—*ethics* and *aesthetics*. Ethics is the study of moral values and conduct. "How should I behave?" is an ethical question. Ethical theory seeks to provide right values as the foundation for right actions. In many ways, ethics is the crucial issue of our times. World societies have made unprecedented technological advances, but have not advanced significantly, if at all, in their ethical and moral conceptions.

Both as individuals and within societies, human beings exist in a world in which they cannot avoid meaningful ethical decisions. Thus schools must teach ethical concepts to their students. The problem is that people embrace different ethical bases and feel quite negatively about having their children indoctrinated in a moral view that is alien to their fundamental beliefs. That fact has put schools at the center of the various culture wars that have rocked society at large.[9] It has also led Adventists and other Christians to establish their own schools. The desire to pass on to their children a specific system of moral values is a powerful motivator for most parents.

At the heart of ethical discussions are such questions as, "Are ethical standards and moral values absolute or relative?" "Do universal moral values exist?" "Can morality be separated from religion?" and "Who or what forms the basis of ethical authority?"

The second major branch of axiology is *aesthetics*. Aesthetics asks such questions as "What is beautiful?" and "What should I like?" Aesthetics is the realm of value that searches for the principles governing the creation and appreciation of beauty and art in both the higher arts and the things of daily life, such as school architecture, television programs, and billboards. Evaluations of beauty and ugliness fall into the aesthetic realm. Thus aesthetic valuation is a part of daily life and cannot be avoided.

The aesthetic experience is tied to the cognitive world of intellectual understanding, but also soars beyond the cognitive into the affective realm because of its focus on feeling and emotion. Aesthetic experiences enable people to move beyond the limits imposed by purely rational thought and the inadequacies of human language. A picture, song, or story may create an impression in a person that could never be conveyed through logical argument.

Humans are aesthetic beings; thus it is just as impossible to avoid teaching aesthetics in the school, home, media, or church as it is to avoid inculcating ethical values. However, the realm of aesthetics does not exist in a vacuum. To the contrary, aesthetic belief is directly related to other aspects of people's philosophy. For example, if subjectivity and randomness are embraced in epistemology and metaphysics, they will be reflected in both aesthetics and ethics. People's aesthetic values reflect their total philosophy.

PHILOSOPHIC ISSUES AND EDUCATIONAL GOALS AND PRACTICES

Figure 1 illustrates the relationship between philosophical beliefs and practice. It indicates that a distinct metaphysical and epistemological viewpoint will lead the educator to a value orientation. That orientation, with its corresponding view of reality and truth, will determine what educational goals are deliberately chosen by teachers as they seek to implement their philosophical beliefs in the classroom.

As a consequence, educators' goals suggest appropriate decisions about a variety of areas: students' needs, the teacher's role in the classroom, the most important things to emphasize in the curriculum, the teaching methodologies that will best communicate the curriculum, and the social function of the school. Only when an educator has taken a position on such matters can appropriate policies be implemented.

As Figure 1 indicates, philosophy is not the sole determinant of specific educational practices. Elements in the everyday world (such as political factors, economic conditions, social forces, and expectations of the students' families or community) also play a significant role in shaping and modifying educational practices. However, it is important to realize that philosophy still provides the basic boundaries for educational practice for any given educator in a specific setting.

Only when teachers clearly understand their philosophy and examine and evaluate its implications for daily activity in an Adventist setting can they expect to be effective in reaching their personal goals and those of the schools for which they teach. That is so because, as *Knight's Law* declares: "It is impossible to arrive at your destination unless you know where you are going."

Corollary Number 1 is also important for every teacher and school: "A school [or teacher] that does not come close to attaining its goals will eventually lose its support."

Dissatisfaction occurs when Adventist schools lose their distinctiveness and Adventist teachers fail to understand why their institutions must be unique. Such teachers and schools *should* lose their support, since Adventist education without a clearly understood and

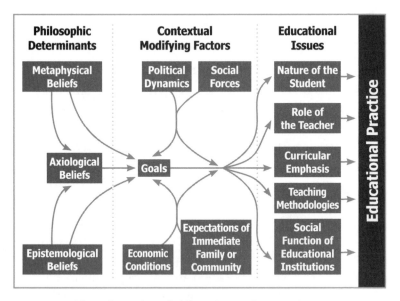

FIGURE 1.   The Relationship of Philosophy to Educational Practice

implemented Adventist philosophy is an impossible contradiction and a waste of money.

Corollary Number 2 is therefore crucial to the health and even the survival of Adventist schools—and the educators in those schools. "We think only when it hurts." In too many places, Adventist education is already hurting. The greatest gifts we as educators can give to the Adventist educational system and to society are (1) to consciously examine our educational philosophy from the perspective of biblical Christianity, (2) to carefully consider the implications of that philosophy for daily classroom activity, and then (3) to implement that philosophy consistently and effectively.

POINTS TO PONDER

- Why study the philosophy of education? What difference(s) should it make?
- Why is metaphysics so important to education?

- Which is more important—epistemology or metaphysics? Why?
- What is it about the field of axiology that makes it explosive in the schools? What are some of the present-day axiological issues that are at the forefront of educational discussion?

Notes

1. David K. Naugle, *Worldview: The History of a Concept* (Grand Rapids, MI: Eerdmans, 2002), 260.

2. Ellen G. White, *Counsels to Parents, Teachers, and Students* (Mountain View, CA: Pacific Press, 1943), 49.

3. Ellen G. White, *Fundamentals of Christian Education* (Nashville: Southern Publishing Association, 1923), 541.

4. Van Cleve Morris, *Philosophy and the American School* (Boston: Houghton Mifflin, 1961), 19–20.

5. For a helpful treatment of the various "isms," see Norman L. Geisler and William D. Watkins, *Worlds Apart: A Handbook on World Views,* 2nd ed. (Grand Rapids, MI: Baker, 1989); a broader treatment is found in James W. Sire, *The Universe Next Door: A Basic Worldview Catalog,* 5th ed. (Downers Grove, IL: InterVarsity, 2009).

6. David Elton Trueblood, *Philosophy of Religion* (New York: Harper and Row, 1957), xiv.

7. Desmond Morris, *The Naked Ape* (New York: Dell, 1967).

8. David Elton Trueblood, *A Place to Stand* (New York: Harper and Row, 1969), 22. For a fuller discussion on the limits of proof, see Trueblood's *General Philosophy* (New York: Harper and Row, 1963), 92–111.

9. See James Davison Hunter, *Culture Wars: The Struggle to Define America* (New York: Basic Books, 1991); Jonathan Zimmerman, *Whose America? Culture Wars in the Public Schools* (Cambridge, MA: Harvard University Press, 2002).

An Adventist Approach to Philosophy

Chapter 1 highlighted the most important philosophic issues and how they relate to education. This one will examine each of those issues and their educational implications from a distinctively Christian/Adventist perspective.

TOWARD A CHRISTIAN METAPHYSICS

The most fundamental and inescapable observation facing every human being is the reality and mystery of personal existence in a complex environment. Atheistic philosopher Jean-Paul Sartre raised that issue when he noted that the basic philosophic problem is that something is there, rather than that nothing is there. Francis Schaeffer, reflecting upon that insight, wrote that "nothing that is worth calling a philosophy can sidestep the question of the fact that things do exist and that they exist in their present form and complexity."[1]

Complexity is a key word in that sentence. Yet despite the complexity of existence, it does seem to be intelligible. Humans do not live in a universe gone mad or one behaving erratically. To the contrary, the world around us and the universe at large apparently operate according to consistent laws that can be discovered, communicated, and used in making trustworthy predictions. Modern science is predicated upon that predictability.

Another thing about our world is that it is basically friendly to humans and other forms of life. If it were intrinsically hostile, life would most certainly be extinguished by the ceaseless assault of an unfriendly environment upon relatively feeble organisms. The natural world appears to be made-to-order to provide food, water, temperature, light, and a host of other necessities that are essential to the continuation of life. The parameters of the conditions necessary for the maintenance of life are quite narrow, and even small changes in the availability of life's essentials would threaten the existence of life as we know it. Thus the continuing existence of life points to a basically friendly universe.

But is it *really* friendly? Clearly, one doesn't have to be especially brilliant to realize that many things are wrong with our world. We daily observe a beautiful world seemingly made for life and happiness, but filled with animosity, deterioration, and death. We are faced with the seemingly intractable problem of pain and death existing in the midst of orderliness and life. There appears to be a great controversy between the forces of good and the forces of evil that manifests itself in every aspect of life. The universe may be friendly toward life, but there is no denying that it is often antagonistic to peace, orderliness, and even life itself. Humanity's habitat is not a place of neutrality. Rather, it is often an arena of active conflict.

The problem we face is making sense of the complex world in which we live. The almost universal longing of human beings to make sense of their world has led them to ask those questions that form the heart of philosophy.

Some people believe that there is no ultimate meaning to existence. But others find it less than satisfactory to suggest that intelligence flows out of ignorance, order out of chaos, personality out of impersonality, and something out of nothing. It seems more likely that an infinite universe postulates an infinite Creator, an intelligent and orderly universe points to an ultimate Intelligence, a basically friendly universe points to a benevolent Being, and the human personality reflects a Personality upon which individual personalities are modeled. People refer to this infinite Creator, ultimate Intelligence, benevolent Being, and original Personality as "god," while at the same time realizing that this word is meaningless until it is defined.

But how to define *god* becomes a very real problem, especially when we acknowledge the mental limitations of the human race. Not only are we faced with our serious ignorance of the complexities of our immediate environment, but also with our inability even to begin to cope with the apparent infinity of time, space, and complexity in the universe at large. And obviously, if we have difficulty grasping the complexity of the creation, we have an even greater challenge in understanding the Creator, since a maker must be more complex and greater than that which is made.

And that reality brings us to the jagged frontier between metaphysics and epistemology. Because of our innate human inability to understand the complex reality of the world in which we live, the Creator-God has seen fit to provide a revelation of Himself, His world, and the human predicament in the Bible.

"In the beginning God" (Gen. 1:1) are the very first words of the Bible. With those words, we find the ultimate foundation of an Adventist approach to metaphysics. Everything else is secondary to God's existence. God is the reason for everything else. And if God is central to the Bible and reality itself, He must also be at the center of education. An education that leaves God out of its program is of necessity inadequate. How could it be adequate if it leaves out of its approach to learning this most important fact?

But God not only exists, He also acts. Thus the Bible's first verse continues with these words: "God created the heavens and the earth." The material world as we know it did not come about by accident. Rather, its intricacies reflect both design and a Designer. Genesis tells us that God did not create a flawed world, but one that He could call "very good" near the end of creation week (Gen. 1:31).

Two things are noteworthy about that "very good" statement. The first is that God created a perfect world. The second is that the material world is inherently good and valuable and not, as held by some forms of Greek philosophy, an evil aspect of reality. According to the biblical view, the physical environment we inhabit should be respected and cared for because it is God's good creation.

The final act in creation week was the establishment of a memorial that would remind humans of who God is and what He has done. "Thus," we read, "the heavens and the earth were finished, and all the host of them. And on the seventh day God finished his work which he had done, and he rested on the seventh day from all his work which he had done. So God blessed the seventh day and hallowed it, because on it God rested from all his work which he had done in creation" (Gen. 2:1–3).

The Sabbath is one of the first educational features in Genesis. A weekly object lesson, its observance by humans was enshrined in the Fourth Commandment (Exod. 20:8–11) and is relevant throughout human history. One of the final messages to be given to earth's inhabitants before the second coming of Jesus is to "'worship him who made heaven and earth, the sea and the fountains of water'" (Rev. 14:7), an obvious reference back to the Ten Commandments and through them to the memorial of Creation in Genesis 2.

Central to Christian metaphysics are the facts that God exists and that He acted in creation. But He not only created birds and trees, He also created human beings in His own image (Gen. 1:26, 27). Of all God's creatures, human beings are the only ones made in the image of God. Thus in its original state, humanity was sinless and pure. Beyond that, humans were created in a responsible relationship to their Maker. God gave them "dominion" over every living creature and "all the earth" (v. 26). Human beings were created to be God's stewards, His vice-regents on earth.

A fourth important element in a Christian understanding of reality is the "invention" of sin by Lucifer, who forgot his own creatureliness and sought to put himself in the place of God (Isa. 14:12–14; Ezek. 28:14–17). With the entrance of sin, we find the genesis of the controversy between good and evil that we experience in the world around us.

Sin is bad enough in the abstract. But, the Bible tells us, it didn't just remain out there in the universe. Rather, Lucifer spread it to earth. How sin entered planet Earth and the human race is set forth in Genesis 3, which describes the corruption of humanity as a result of what theologians call "the Fall."

The effects of sin have been devastating to the human race. Not only did sin cause estrangement between God and humans (Gen. 3:8–11), humans and their fellow beings (v. 12), humans with their own selves (v. 13), and humans with God's created world (vv. 17, 18), but it also led to death (v. 19) and a partial loss of the image of God (Gen. 5:3; 9:6; James 3:9).

Accompanying the invention of sin by Lucifer and its spread to humanity at the Fall is the reality of the ongoing conflict between Christ and Satan (often referred to as the "Great Controversy") that began before the creation of this earth and will not be terminated until the final destruction of the devil and his works at the end of the millennium (Rev. 20:11–15). That controversy dominates the pages of the Bible from Genesis 3 through Revelation 20. The focal point of this warfare is Satan's attempt to discredit God's character and to pervert human perceptions of His law of love (Matt. 22:36–40; Rom. 13:8–10). God's foremost exhibition of His love was not only sending Jesus to rescue a fallen race but more particularly Christ's death on the cross. The Book of Revelation indicates that God's law of love will be an issue in the controversy between the forces of good and evil until the end of earthly history (12:17; 14:12).

The Fall in Genesis 3 is a central tenet of the biblical worldview. Without the Fall, the rest of the Bible makes no sense. Starting with Genesis 3, the Bible features both the results of human transgression and God's plan and efforts for dealing with the sin problem. As we will see when we discuss the needs of students, the Fall and its results are foundational issues in Christian education. They are, in fact, issues that make Christian education unique among history's educational philosophies.

Another aspect of a Christian metaphysics is the inability of human beings, without divine aid, to change their own nature, overcome their inherent sinfulness, or restore the lost image of God. *Lost* is the word the Bible uses to describe the human condition. The daily news reflects the results of that lostness in its continuous reporting of greed, perversion, and violence. And if the news were not enough, popular entertainment focuses on illicit sex and violence. The Bible describes the same problems as occurring even among God's heroes.

Of course, ever since the Fall, there have been people who have wanted nothing to do with God and His principles. But many humans have wanted to be good. Among them are those who make long lists of resolutions and attempt to live flawless lives, but to no avail. They repeatedly experience failure as their passions, appetites, greed, and natural inclination toward selfishness overcome their best intentions; and they repeat the dynamics of the Fall in a personal fall into sinful ways. Another group have achieved a fair amount of goodness or respectability through self-control and law keeping, but have ended up being proud of their righteousness. Included in this group are the Pharisees throughout the ages who smugly declare that they are better than other people, not recognizing their own blindness to their real condition (Luke 18:9–14). No matter how hard human beings try to be righteous, they still remain lost and confused.

As a result of universal human lostness in its several variations, the Bible pictures God taking the initiative for humanity's salvation and restoration through the incarnation, life, death, resurrection, and heavenly ministry of Jesus Christ. Evidence of God's initiative in the rescue plan of salvation appears throughout the Bible. We first find that initiative in Genesis 3:9, but it runs throughout the Old Testament and into the New, where we are told that "God so loved the world that He *gave* his only Son, that whoever believes in him should not perish but have eternal life" (John 3:16). Jesus put it somewhat differently when He claimed that His mission was "'to seek and to save the lost'" (Luke 19:10).

An important aspect of Christ's incarnation is that it reveals God's character. "In many and various ways," we read in the opening words of the Book of Hebrews, "God spoke of old to our fathers by the prophets; but in these last days he has spoken to us by a Son, whom he appointed the heir of all things, through whom also he created the world. He reflects the glory of God and bears the very stamp of his nature" (1:1–3). Jesus is the fullest revelation of God's character. The Bible declares that "God is love" (1 John 4:8), but reading those parts of it that make Him appear to be less than loving makes us wonder about His real nature. The earthly life of Jesus, however, illustrates God's love and epitomizes the other attributes of His character. As a result, Jesus's character and life provide an ethical ideal for His followers.

Because of human lostness, God sent the Holy Spirit to implement His plan for restoring His image in fallen humanity. That work includes the calling out of a community of believers. The Bible pictures the rescue of the lost as a divine act in which individuals are born of the Spirit (John 3:3–6), transformed in their minds and hearts (Rom. 12:2), and resurrected to a new way of life in which they model Christ's character (Rom. 6:1–14). Each of those acts results from the work of the Holy Spirit, the third Person of the Godhead.

Those who respond positively to the Spirit's work become a part of the community of saints which the Bible calls the Church or the body of Christ (Eph. 1:22, 23). But we must not confuse the Church and the church. The visible church on Earth is made up of members who may or may not be under the guidance of the Spirit. But the Church of God includes only those believers who have truly surrendered their hearts to God and have been born of the Spirit, who is central to God's great plan of rescuing the lost and restoring the divine ideals.

Some of those ideals relate to social action. God commands His people to feed the hungry, care for the sick, and seek in all ways not only to preserve the Earth but also to make it a better place. But in the end, He knows that even the best human efforts at reform will fall short of what needs to be done to clean up the mess created by sin.

Thus, social action is an important function of God's people, but an inadequate one in the sense of eradicating the problem.

As a result, Christ has promised to return at the end of earthly history to put an end to sin and its results. At that time, He will not only feed the hungry but also abolish hunger, not only comfort the grieving but also eradicate death. The Bible pictures the Second Advent as the hope of the ages (Titus 2:13; Rev. 21:1–4). It describes the final act in the drama of salvation as the restoration of Planet Earth and its inhabitants to their Edenic condition (2 Pet. 3:10–13). The Bible closes with a picture of the restored Earth and an invitation for people to join God and Christ in their great plan of redemption and restoration (Rev. 21, 22).

Summary of the Biblical Framework of Reality

- The existence of the living God, the Creator.
- The creation by God of a perfect world and universe.
- Humanity's creation in the image of God as His responsible agents on earth.
- The invention of sin by Lucifer, who forgot his own creatureliness and sought to put himself in the place of God.
- The spread of sin to the earth by Lucifer, resulting in the Fall of humanity and the partial loss of God's image.
- The conflict or Great Controversy between Christ and Satan over the character of God and His law of love, which runs throughout earthly history.
- The inability of human beings, without divine aid, to change their own nature, overcome their inherent sinfulness, or restore the lost image of God within themselves.
- The initiative of God for humanity's salvation and its restoration to its original state through the incarnation, life, death, resurrection, and heavenly ministry of Jesus Christ.
- The revelation of God's character in the life and teachings of Christ, which provides the foundation for Christian ethics.
- The activity of the Holy Spirit in the plan for restoring God's

image in fallen humanity and His work in the calling out of the community of believers, the Church.

- The command of Christ for the Church to be socially active in the interim between His first and second advents.
- The return of Christ at the end of earthly history to put an end to sin and solve the problems that human social action could not eradicate.
- The eventual restoration of the earth and its faithful inhabitants to the Edenic condition.

Metaphysics and Adventist Education

The above discussion presents the basic outline of a biblical view of reality. Because Christianity is a supernatural religion, it is thoroughly antithetical to all forms of naturalism, to those theistic schemes that do not place God at the center of the human educational experience, and to humanism, which purports that humanity can save itself through its own wisdom and goodness. Adventist education, to be Christian in actuality and not so in name only, must consciously be built upon a biblical metaphysical position.

A Christian view of metaphysics provides the foundation for Adventist education. Christian educational systems have been established because God exists and because His existence sheds light on the meaning of every aspect of life. Other educational systems have alternative foundations and cannot be substituted for Christian education. Belief in the Christian view of reality motivates people to sacrifice both their time and their means for the establishment of Christian schools. The same is true for Adventist education, which not only sets forth those teachings that it shares with other Christians, but also those biblical beliefs that make the Seventh-day Adventist Church a distinct Christian movement with an end-time message to share with the world. Adventist schools that teach only those beliefs that the denomination shares with other Christians have no reason for existing.

A biblical metaphysic determines what shall be studied in the school, and the contextual framework in which every subject is presented. As such, the biblical view of reality supplies the criteria for curricular selection and emphasis. The biblically based curriculum has a unique emphasis because of Christianity's unique metaphysical viewpoint. Adventist education must treat all subject matter from the perspective of the biblical worldview. Every course must be formulated in terms of its relationship to the existence and purpose of the Creator God.

Thus, every aspect of Adventist education is determined by the biblical view of reality. Biblical metaphysical presuppositions not only justify and determine the existence of, curriculum used in, and social role of Adventist education; they also explicate the nature, needs, and potential of the learner, suggest the most beneficial types of relationships between teachers and their students, and provide criteria for the selection of teaching methodologies. Those topics will be further developed in chapters 3–7.

AN ADVENTIST EPISTEMOLOGICAL PERSPECTIVE

Epistemology, as we noted above, deals with how a person knows. As such, it has to do with one of the most basic problems of human existence. If our epistemology is incorrect, then it follows that everything else in our philosophic understanding will be wrong or, at the very least, distorted. We earlier saw that every philosophic system develops a hierarchy of epistemological sources that becomes foundational.

For Christians, God's revelation in the Bible is the foremost source of knowledge and the most essential epistemological authority. All other sources of knowledge must be tested and verified in the light of Scripture. Underlying the authoritative role of the Bible are several assumptions:

- Humans exist in a supernatural universe in which the infinite Creator God has revealed Himself to finite minds on a level they can comprehend in at least a limited fashion.
- Human beings were created in the image of God, and even though fallen, are capable of rational thought.

- Communication with other intelligent beings (people and God) is possible in spite of humanity's inherent limitations and the inadequacies of human language.

- The God who cared enough to reveal Himself to people also cared enough to protect the essence of that revelation as it was transmitted through succeeding generations.

- Human beings are able to make sufficiently correct interpretations of the Bible through the guidance of the Holy Spirit to arrive at valid truth.

The Bible is an authoritative source of Truths that are beyond the possibility of attainment except through revelation. This source of knowledge deals with the big questions, such as the meaning of life and death, where the world came from and what its future will be, how the problem of sin arose and how it is being dealt with, and the like. The purpose of Scripture is to "instruct" people "for salvation through faith in Christ." Beyond that, it is "profitable for teaching, for reproof, for correction, and for training in righteousness" (2 Tim. 3:15, 16). It should be apparent, then, that the Bible is not an exhaustive source of knowledge and never was intended to be a divine encyclopedia. It leaves many questions unanswered. On the other hand, because it answers the most basic questions of finite humanity, it provides a perspective and a metaphysical framework in which to explore unanswered questions and to arrive at coherent, unified answers.

The Bible does not try to justify its claims, and thus must be accepted by faith based upon both external and internal evidences, such as the discoveries of archaeology, the witness of fulfilled prophecy, and the satisfaction its way of life brings to the human heart. Reinforcing this idea, we read in *Steps to Christ* that "God never asks us to believe, without giving sufficient evidence upon which to base our faith. His existence, His character, the truthfulness of His word, are all established by testimony that appeals to our reason; and this testimony is abundant. Yet God has never removed the possibility of doubt. Our faith must rest upon evidence, not demonstration. Those who wish to doubt will have opportunity; while those who really desire to know the truth will find plenty of evidence on which to rest their faith."[2]

Seventh-day Adventists believe that the Bible teaches that the prophetic gift will be in the church until the Second Advent (Eph. 4:8, 11–13) and that Christians are not to reject the claims of those who believe they have the prophetic gift, but to test their teachings by the testimony of the Bible (see Matt. 7:15–20; 1 Thess. 5:19–21; 1 John 4:1, 2).

Having done that testing, the Seventh-day Adventist Church early concluded that Ellen G. White had a valid gift of revelatory prophecy for the Adventist community that would help it to be faithful to biblical principles during the period before the Second Advent. That gift was not given to take the place of the Bible or to provide new doctrines, but to help God's people understand and apply God's Word as revealed in the Bible. "The written testimonies," Ellen White penned, "are not to give new light, but to impress vividly upon the heart the truths of inspiration already revealed. Man's duty to God and to his fellow man has been distinctly specified in God's word, yet but few of you are obedient to the light given. Additional truth is not brought out; but God has through the *Testimonies* simplified the great truths already given and in His own chosen way brought them before the people to awaken and impress the mind with them."[3]

It is important to note that Ellen White had a great deal to say about education in the context of the biblical worldview. As a result, we will quote her insights where they contribute to rounding out an Adventist philosophy of education. The source of knowledge next in importance for the Christian is that of nature as people encounter it in daily life and through scientific study. The world around us is a revelation of the Creator God (Ps. 19:1–4; Rom. 1:20). Theologians have given the term *special revelation* to the Scriptures, while they have viewed the natural world as a *general revelation*.

Regarding the relationship between special and general revelation, Ellen White writes: "Since the book of nature and the book of revelation bear the impress of the same master mind, they cannot but speak in harmony. By different methods, and in different languages, they witness to the same great truths. Science is ever discovering new wonders; but she brings from her research nothing that, rightly understood, conflicts with divine revelation. The book of nature and the written word shed light upon each other. They make us acquainted with God by teaching us something of the laws through which He works."[4]

Yet even the casual observer soon discovers problems in interpreting the book of nature. He or she sees not only love and life, but also hate and death. The natural world, as observed by fallible humanity, gives a garbled and seemingly contradictory message concerning ultimate reality. The apostle Paul noted that the whole of creation has been affected by the Fall (Rom. 8:22). The effects of the controversy between good and evil have made general revelation by itself an insufficient source of knowledge about God and ultimate reality. The findings of science and the daily experiences of life must be interpreted in the light of scriptural revelation, which supplies the framework for epistemological interpretation.[5]

The study of nature does enrich humanity's understanding of its environment. It also provides answers for some of the many questions not dealt with in the Bible. However, the investigative value of human science must not be overestimated. As Frank Gaebelein points out, scientific people have not produced the truth of science. They have merely uncovered or found what is already there. The hunches gained through patient scientific research that lead to a further grasp of truth are not mere luck. They are a part of God's disclosure of truth to humanity through the natural world.[6]

A third epistemological source for the Christian is rationality. Humans, having been created in the image of God, possess a rational nature. They can think abstractly, be reflective, and reason from cause to effect. As a result of the Fall, human reasoning powers have been lessened but not destroyed. God's plea to sinful individuals is that they might "reason together" with Him concerning the human predicament and its solution (Isa. 1:18).

The role of rationalism in Christian epistemology must be clearly defined. The Christian faith is not a rationalistic production. People do not arrive at Christian truth through developing by themselves a system of thought that leads to a correct view of God, humanity, and the nature of sin and salvation. Rather, Christianity is a revealed religion. Unaided human reason can be deceitful and lead away from truth. Christians, therefore, while not rationalistic in the fullest sense of the word, are rational. Bernard Ramm has correctly remarked that reason is not a source of religious authority, but rather a mode of apprehending truth. As such, "it is the truth apprehended which is authoritative, not reason."[7]

The rational aspect of epistemology is an essential part in, but not the sole element of, knowing. It helps us understand truth obtained through special and general revelation, and enables us to extend that knowledge into the unknown. In a Christian epistemology, the findings of reason must always be checked against the truth of Scripture. The same principle must be applied to knowledge gained through intuition and from the study of authorities. The all-encompassing epistemological test is to compare all purported truth to the scriptural framework.

In closing, we need to make several other observations about a Christian approach to epistemology:

- From the biblical perspective, all truth is God's truth, since truth finds its source in God as the Creator and Originator.[8]
- There is a Great Controversy underway in the area of epistemology, just as there is a similar tension in nature. The forces of evil are continually seeking to undermine the Bible, distort human reasoning, and convince people to rely on their own inadequate fallen selves in their search for truth. The epistemological conflict is of crucial importance because misdirection in this area will shift every other human endeavor off-center.
- There are absolute Truths in the universe, but fallen humans can gain only a relative or imperfect grasp of those absolutes.
- The Bible is not concerned with abstract truth. It pictures truth as related to life. Knowing, in the fullest biblical sense, means applying perceived knowledge to one's daily life.

- The various sources of knowledge available to the Christian are complementary. Thus, while all sources can and should be used by the Christian, each one should be evaluated in the light of the biblical pattern.

- The acceptance of a Christian epistemology cannot be separated from the acceptance of a Christian metaphysics, and vice versa.

The Christian view of truth, along with Christian metaphysics, lies at the foundation of the very existence of Adventist education. The acceptance of revelation as the basic source of authority places the Bible at the heart of Christian education and provides the knowledge framework within which all subject matters are to be evaluated. That insight impacts the curriculum in a particular way. We will see in our later discussion of curriculum that the biblical revelation provides both the foundation and the context for all subjects taught in Christian schools. Christian epistemology, since it deals with the way people come to know anything, also influences the selection and application of teaching methodologies.

ASPECTS OF CHRISTIAN AXIOLOGY

Christian values build directly upon a biblical perspective of metaphysics and epistemology. Both a Christian ethic and a Christian aesthetic are grounded in the biblical doctrine of creation. Ethical and aesthetic values exist because the Creator deliberately created a world with those dimensions. Thus the principles of Christian axiology are derived from the Bible, which in its ultimate sense is a revelation of the character and values of God.

A crucial consideration in a Christian axiology is that Christian metaphysics sets forth a position of radical discontinuity from other worldviews, in terms of the normality of the present world order. While most non-Christians believe that the present condition of humanity and earthly affairs is the normal state of things, the Bible teaches that human beings have fallen from their normal relationship to God, other people, their own selves, and the world around them. From the biblical perspective, sin and its results have altered people's nature and affected their ideals and valuing processes. As a result of the present world's abnormality, people often value the wrong things. Beyond that, they are liable to call evil "good" and good "evil" because of their faulty frame of reference.

Christ Himself was an axiological radical. His radicalism stemmed in part from the fact that He believed humanity's true home is heaven and not earth. But He did not teach that the present life is not of value. Rather, He claimed that there are things of more value, and that they should be the foundation for human activity. When one applies Christ's teaching, his or her life will be based upon a different set of values from the lives of persons who feel at home in the abnormal world of sin. To be normal in terms of embracing God's ideals will therefore make a Christian appear abnormal by the standards of the present social order.

Ethics

Christian values must be built upon Christian principles. Thus, they are not merely an extension of non-Christian values, even though there are certainly areas of overlap. As noted earlier, the two major subsets of axiology are ethics (the realm of the good) and aesthetics (the realm of the beautiful). The absolute basis of Christian ethics is God. There is no standard or law beyond God. Law, as it is revealed in Scripture, is based upon God's character, which centers on love and justice (Exod. 34:6, 7; 1 John 4:8; Rev. 16:7; 19:2). Biblical history provides examples of divine love and justice in action.

The concept of love is a meaningless idea until it is defined. The Christian looks to the Bible for a definition, because it is there that the God who is love has revealed Himself in a concrete way that is understandable to human minds. The Bible's fullest elucidations of the meaning of love appear in the actions and attitudes expressed by Jesus, the exposition of love in 1 Corinthians 13, and in the underlying meaning of the Ten Commandments. Even a brief study reveals a distinct qualitative difference between what "normal" humans refer to as love and the biblical concept of divine love. John Powell captured the essence of divine love when he pointed out that love focuses on giving rather than receiving.[9] It works for the very best good of others, even those thought of as enemies. In that same vein, Carl Henry has aptly written that "Christian ethics is an ethics of service."[10] Thus it is that Christian ethics and Christian love stand in radical discontinuity from what is generally thought of as love by human beings.

That concept leads us to the ethical expression of God through His revealed law. All too many Christians believe that God's basic law is the Ten Commandments. That is not the position Jesus took. When asked about the greatest law, He replied that "'You shall love the Lord your God with all your heart, and with all your soul, and with all your mind. This is the great and first commandment. And a second is like it, You shall love your neighbor as yourself. On these two command-ments depend all the law and the prophets'" (Matt. 22:37–40). The Ten Commandments thus are an extension and concrete illustration of the Law of Love. The first four commandments explain a person's duties in regard to love to God, while the last six explain various aspects of a person's love for other human beings (see Rom. 13:8–10). In one sense, the Ten Commandments may be seen as a negative ver-sion of the Law of Love, explained in a way that gives people some definite guidelines that they can apply to daily life.

One of the difficulties with a negative ethical base is that people are always seeking to know when they can stop loving their neighbor, when the limit has been reached. Peter's question in regard to the lim-its of forgiveness is a case in point. Like most individuals, Peter was more interested in when he could stop loving his neighbors than in how he could continue to love them. Christ's seventy-times-seven answer indicates that there are no limits to love (Matt. 18:21–35). There is never a time when we can stop loving and cut loose to be our "real selves." That is the message of Christ's two great commandments.

Thus, the Christian ethical perspective is primarily positive rather than negative. That is, Christian ethics focuses primarily on a life of loving action and only secondarily on what we should avoid. Christian growth does not come from what we don't do, but is rather a product of what we actively do in our daily lives. And that positive ethic is based upon the new birth experience (John 3:3–6). Christians have not only died to the old way of life; they have also been resurrected to a new way of life as they walk with Christ (Rom. 6:1–11).

Before concluding our discussion of Christian ethics, there are several more points to make. One is that a biblical ethic is internal rather than external. Jesus for example, remarked that harboring thoughts of hate or adultery is just as immoral as the acts themselves (Matt. 5:21–28). He also taught that all external actions flow out of the heart and mind (Matt. 15:18, 19).

Second, the Christian ethic is based upon a personal relationship with both God and other people. It involves actually loving both God and people and cannot be satisfied with a mere legal and/or mechanical relationship. Of course, our relationships with others should be legal, but beyond that, they must also be personal.

Third, the biblical ethic is based upon the fact that every individual is created in the image of God and can reason from cause to effect and make moral decisions. They can choose to do good or evil. Thus, the Christian ethic is a moral enterprise. Unthinking morality is a contradiction in terms.

Fourth, Christian morality is not merely concerned with people's basic needs. It wants the very best for them.

Fifth, a Christian ethic, contrary to many people's perspective, is not something that interferes with the good life. "In reality, moral rules are directions for running the human machine. Every moral rule is there to prevent a breakdown, or a strain, or a friction, in the running of that machine."[11]

Sixth, the function of the Christian ethic is redemptive and restorative. Because of the Fall, human beings became alienated from God, other people, their own selves, and their physical environment. The role of ethics is to enable people to live in a way that helps to restore those relationships and to bring people into the position of wholeness for which they were created.

Aesthetics

The second major branch of axiology is aesthetics. It is an important function of all educational systems to develop in students a healthy sense of what is beautiful and what is ugly. What is a Christian aesthetic? To arrive at a definition, several points need to be made. The first is that humans are, by their very nature, aesthetic beings. They not only appreciate beauty, but also seem to be compulsive creators of it. That is one result of their having been created in the image of God. God not only created functional things—He also created things of beauty. He could have created the world destitute of pleasing colors, without the sweet scents of flowers, or the amazing array of birds and animals. The existence of beauty in nature says something about the Creator. Of course, one difference between the creatorship of people and that of God is that He created out of nothing (Heb. 11:3), while humans in their finiteness must fashion and mold that which already exists.

A second point to note is that while creativity is good, not everything that humans create is good, beautiful, or edifying. That is true because even though human beings were created in the image of God, they have fallen and now have a distorted view of reality, truth, and value. Art forms, therefore, not only reveal truth, beauty, and goodness, but also illustrate the unnatural, erroneous, and perverted. Because the galactic controversy between good and evil has invaded every aspect of human life, it also affects the aesthetic realm and is especially powerful in the arts due to their emotional impact and their profound involvement in the intricacies of human existence.

A leading question in the area of Christian aesthetics is whether the subject matter of artistic forms should deal only with the good and beautiful, or whether it should also include the ugly and the grotesque. Using the Bible as a model, we perceive that it does not deal only with the good and the beautiful. But neither does it glorify the ugly and evil. Rather, sin, evil, and ugliness are put in perspective and used to point out humanity's desperate need of a Savior and a better way. In summary, the relationship between the good and the ugly in the Bible is treated realistically so that the Christian, with the eyes of faith, learns to hate the ugly because of his or her relationship with the God who is beauty, truth, and goodness.

Dealing with the relationship between the beautiful and the ugly in art forms is vital to Christian aesthetics because of Paul's warning that by beholding we become changed (2 Cor. 3:18). Aesthetics has a bearing on ethics. What we read, see, hear, and touch has an effect on our daily lives. Aesthetics, therefore, lies at the very center of the Christian life and a religious system of education. As a result, a Christian producer of art (which in one sense is all of us) ideally is a responsible servant of God who, out of a heart filled with Christian love, functions "to make life better, more worthwhile, to create the sound, the shape, the tale, the decoration, the environment that is meaningful and lovely and a joy to mankind."[12]

Perhaps that which is most beautiful from a Christian perspective is whatever contributes toward restoring individuals to a right relationship to their Maker, other people, their own selves, and the environment in which they live. Whatever obstructs the restorative process is, by definition, evil and ugly. The ultimate goal of Christian aesthetics is the creation of a beautiful character.

Axiology and Adventist Education

"Education," Arthur Holmes writes, "has to do with the transmission of values."[13] It is that truism that places axiology alongside of metaphysics and epistemology as a foundational reason why Seventh-day Adventists have chosen to establish and maintain a separate system of schools.

A Christian perspective on such axiological issues as ethics and aesthetics is an essential contribution of Adventist education in a world that has lost a balanced and healthy biblical orientation. The cultural tension in differing value systems is central to what David Naugle labels "worldview warfare."[14] James D. Hunter and Jonathan Zimmerman explore the explosive implications of those axiological issues in books with such expressive titles as *Culture Wars: The Struggle to Define America* and *Whose America? Culture Wars in the Public Schools.*

Values education is a central reason for the existence of Adventist schools. And Adventist educators need to be both informed and active as they seek to transmit to their students a biblically based approach to values.

ADVENTIST PHILOSOPHY AND EDUCATION

The existence of Adventist schools is no accident. To the contrary, the church early in its history realized that because its philosophy differed significantly from other segments of society, it had a responsibility to pass on that philosophy to young people through the development of an educational system. That was a conscious choice built upon philosophic principle. The result has been the creation of an Adventist system of education that currently has more than 8,000 schools, colleges, and universities.

That system and the expense undergirding it can be justified only if the church's schools are faithful to the philosophic foundation upon which they were established. The best way, in the descriptive language of Shane Anderson, "to kill Adventist education" is to neglect those philosophic underpinnings.[15] For that reason alone, the study of the philosophy of Adventist education is of crucial importance to educators, school board members, pastors, and parents.

Thus far in our presentation we have examined the biblical philosophic position that must inform Adventist educational practice. In chapters 3–7 we will discuss what that philosophy means in terms of the needs of the student, the role of the teacher, the formation of the curriculum, the selection of teaching strategies, and the social function of the Adventist school in the church and the larger world.

POINTS TO PONDER

- If you were to define what might be called the "absolute core" of Christian metaphysics, what five points would you select and in what order? Explain your answer.

- What are the implications of epistemology for a Christian school?
- In two or three sentences, highlight the most basic principles underlying a Christian ethic.
- What are the implications of aesthetics for the Adventist school?

Notes

1. Francis A. Schaeffer, *He Is There and He Is Not Silent* (Wheaton, IL: Tyndale House, 1972), 1.
2. Ellen G. White, *Steps to Christ* (Mountain View, CA: Pacific Press, 1956), 105.
3. Ellen G. White, *Testimonies for the Church*, vol. 5 (Mountain View, CA: Pacific Press, 1948), 665.
4. Ellen G. White, *Education* (Mountain View, CA: Pacific Press, 1952), 128.
5. See ibid., 134.
6. Frank E. Gaebelein, "Toward a Philosophy of Christian Education," in *An Introduction to Evangelical Christian Education*, ed. J. Edward Hakes (Chicago: Moody, 1964), 44.
7. Bernard Ramm, *The Pattern of Religious Authority* (Grand Rapids, MI: Eerdmans, 1959), 44.
8. See Arthur F. Holmes, *All Truth Is God's Truth* (Grand Rapids, MI: Eerdmans, 1977), 8–15.
9. John Powell, *The Secret of Staying in Love* (Niles, IL: Argus Communications, 1974), 44, 48.
10. Carl F. H. Henry, *Christian Personal Ethics* (Grand Rapids, MI: Eerdmans, 1957), 219.
11. C. S. Lewis, *Mere Christianity* (New York: Macmillan, 1960), 69.
12. H. R. Rookmaaker, *Modern Art and the Death of a Culture*, 2nd ed. (Downers Grove, IL: InterVarsity, 1973), 243.
13. Arthur F. Holmes, *Shaping Character: Moral Education in the Christian College* (Grand Rapids, MI: Eerdmans, 1991), vii.
14. Naugle, *Worldview*, xvii.
15. Shane Anderson, *How to Kill Adventist Education (and How to Give It a Fighting Chance!)* (Hagerstown, MD: Review and Herald, 2009).

Part II

Implications of Philosophy
for Adventist Education

CHAPTER 3

The Nature of the Student and the Reason for Adventist Education

The need to implement a biblical/Christian/Adventist philosophy in Seventh-day Adventist schools ought to be obvious. But all too often that synthesis is not evident in the schools themselves or in the practice of the professional educators who operate them. Addressing that point in the context of Lutheran education, one of the principal speakers at a meeting of the Association of Lutheran College Faculties observed that the denomination's American colleges "operated according to no distinctive Lutheran or even Christian philosophy of education, but had simply imitated secular patterns to which they had added chapel services, religion classes, and a religious 'atmosphere.'"[1]

That observation, unfortunately, also describes a number of Adventist schools. All too often, Adventist education has not intentionally been built upon a distinctively Adventist philosophy. As a result, many of the church's schools have offered something less than Adventist education and have thereby failed to achieve the purpose for which they were established.

Philosopher Gordon Clark once noted that what goes by the name of Christian education is sometimes a program of "pagan education with a chocolate coating of Christianity." He added that it is the pill, not the coating, that works.[2] Adventist education tends to suffer from this problem as well. Adventist educators and the institutions they serve need to conduct a thorough and ongoing examination, evaluation, and correction of their educational practices to ensure that they align with the church's basic philosophic beliefs. This book will help you flesh out a basis for that ongoing evaluation and orientation.[3]

While the chapters focus on Adventist education in the school, much of the content can be applied within the framework of the home and church since parents and church workers are also educators. The home, the church, and the school all deal with the same children, who have the same nature and needs in the several different venues of their education. Furthermore, the home and church have a curriculum, a teaching style, and a social function akin to that of the school. There is a great need for parents, church workers, and professional educators to gain greater insight into the interdependent nature of their educative functions and to develop effective ways to communicate and reinforce one another's work. A collaboration between the Adventist teacher in the school and Adventist teachers in the home and church is important because *Adventist education is more than Adventist schooling*. The home, church, and school are entrusted with the responsibility of working with the most valuable things on earth, God's children, and ideally each is founded upon the same principles. Having said that, I need to point out that the educative categories that I will be dealing with in the following pages are consciously tied to schooling rather than to the wider realm of education. However, the same principles are important within the various educative contexts.

THE HEART OF ELLEN WHITE'S EDUCATIONAL PHILOSOPHY

In defining the goals of Adventist education, Ellen White's opening pages in *Education* are as good a place to start as anywhere. One of the most perceptive and important paragraphs in the book is found on the second page. "In order to understand what is comprehended in the work of education," she writes, "we need to consider both [1] the nature of man and [2] the purpose of God in creating him. We need to consider also [3] the change in man's condition through the coming in of a knowledge of evil, and [4] God's plan for still fulfilling His glorious purpose in the education of the human race."[4]

She fleshes out the core of her philosophy of education by refining those four points in the next few paragraphs. First, in reflecting upon human nature, she emphasizes that Adam was created in the image of God—physically, mentally, and spiritually. Second, she highlights the purpose of God in creating human beings as one of constant growth so they would ever "more fully" reflect "the glory of the Creator." To that end, God endowed human beings with capacities that were capable of almost infinite development.

"But," thirdly, she notes in discussing the entrance of sin, "by disobedience this was forfeited. Through sin the divine likeness was marred, and well-nigh obliterated. Man's physical powers were weakened, his mental capacity was lessened, his spiritual vision dimmed."

While those three points are foundational to Ellen White's philosophy of education, it is her fourth and last point that is absolutely crucial and that, for her, fully expresses the primary purpose of education. She notes that, in spite of its rebellion and Fall, "the race was not left without hope. By infinite love and mercy the plan of salvation had been devised, and a life of probation was granted. To restore in man the image of his Maker, to bring him back to the perfection in which he was created, to promote the development of body, mind, and soul, that the divine purpose in his creation might be realized—this was to be the work of redemption. This is the object of education, the great object of life."[5]

Ellen White returns to that theme in the fourth chapter of *Education*, where she describes each person's life as the scene of a microcosmic great controversy between good and evil, and every human being as having a desire for goodness but also possessing a "bent to evil." Building upon her earlier insight that God's image is not totally obliterated in fallen humanity, she notes that every human being "receives some ray of divine light. Not only intellectual but spiritual power, a perception of right, a desire for goodness, exists in every heart. But against these principles there is struggling an antagonistic power." As the heritage of the Edenic Fall, there is within each person's nature an evil force which "unaided, he cannot resist. To withstand this force, to attain that ideal which in his inmost soul he accepts as alone worthy, he can find help in but one power. That power is Christ. Co-operation with that power is man's greatest need. In all educational effort should not this co-operation be the highest aim?"[6]

On the next page, she develops this point a bit more, writing that "in the highest sense the work of education and the work of redemption are one, for in education, as in redemption, 'other foundation can no man lay than that is laid, which is Christ Jesus.' . . . To aid the student in comprehending these principles, and in entering into that relation with Christ which will make them a controlling power in the life, should be the teacher's first effort and his constant aim. The teacher who accepts this aim is in truth a co-worker with Christ, a laborer together with God."[7]

Although she had no formal training as a philosopher, Ellen White hit the pivot point of educational philosophy when she placed the human problem of sin at the very center of the educational enterprise. Illustrative of that insight is Paul Nash's *Models of Man: Explorations in the Western Educational Tradition* and *The Educated Man: Studies in the History of Educational Thought*, which Nash developed in conjunction with two other authors.[8] Both books demonstrate the centrality of views of philosophical anthropology or human nature to all educational philosophies. Exemplifying that point are such chapter titles as "The Planned Man: Skinner," "The Reflective Man: Dewey," "The Communal Man: Marx," and "The Natural Man: Rousseau." Even though the focal point of education ought to be the needs of students, to my knowledge, no one has yet published a synthesized, systematic approach to educational philosophy from the perspective of varying views of the nature and needs of human beings.

It's not difficult to insert Ellen White's philosophy into Nash's framework. The title for his chapter on her would be "The Redeemed Man: Ellen White" ("Redeemed Person" for modern readers). The problem of sin and its cure—redemption and restoration—dominate her approach to education.

That same emphasis, of course, is found in the very framework of Scripture, which begins with humans being created in the image of God with infinite potential, continues with the Fall and the entrance of sin, and moves on to God's great redemptive plan as He seeks through a multitude of agencies to rescue humans from their predicament and to restore them to their lost estate. That sequence represents the plan of the Bible, in which its first two (Gen. 1, 2) and last two chapters (Rev. 21, 22) depict a perfect world. The third chapter from the beginning (Gen. 3) presents the entrance of sin, and the third chapter from the end (Rev. 20) focuses on sin's final destruction. In between, from Genesis 4 through Revelation 19, the Bible sets forth God's plan for redeeming and restoring the fallen race.

Although all these points represent basic Christian doctrine, surprisingly enough, they have too often escaped significant treatment by Christian philosophers of education. In fact, I know of no book that gives them the same centrality as Ellen White's *Education*. Allan Hart Jahsmann's *What's Lutheran in Education?* comes closest, noting in one essay the same basic points as Ellen White and concluding with the dictum that "the first concern of Lutheran education must always be the leading of a people to a conviction of sin and a personal faith in Jesus Christ as the Lamb of God."[9] Unfortunately, Jahsmann's insights on the Fall and the restoration of God's image are not widely represented in evangelical educational theory. But, as noted above, these concepts stand at the very center of Ellen White's understanding of education and are implied in the Bible. It was with those teachings in mind that I wrote some years ago that "*the nature, condition, and needs of the student provide the focal point for Christian educational philosophy and direct educators toward the goals of Christian education.*"[10]

Before moving away from the big picture of Ellen White's understanding of educational philosophy, we need to examine one other statement. *Education*'s very first paragraph presents another foundational pillar in her approach to education. "Our ideas of education," we read, "take too narrow and too low a range. There is need of a broader scope, a higher aim. True education means more than the pursual of a certain course of study. It means more than a preparation for the life that now is. It has to do with the whole being, and with the whole period of existence possible to man. It is the harmonious development of the physical, the mental, and the spiritual powers. It prepares the student for the joy of service in this world and for the higher joy of wider service in the world to come."[11]

The key word in that paragraph is *whole*, a word she uses with two dimensions. First, Adventist education must emphasize the "whole" or entire period of human existence. Thus it is not merely focused on helping students learn how to earn a living or become cultured by the standards of the present world. Those aims may be worthy and important, but they are not sufficient. The realm of eternity and preparation for it must also come under the purview of any Adventist education worthy of church support. On the other hand, some pious but misdirected individuals might be tempted to make heaven the focus of education while neglecting the present realm and preparation for the world of work and participation in human society. Ellen White asserted that neither extreme is correct. Rather, preparation for both the earthly and the eternal worlds must be included in Adventist education and placed in proper relationship to each other.

The second aspect of wholeness in the above paragraph is the imperative to develop the entire person. Adventist education needs to aim at developing all aspects of human beings rather than focusing merely on the intellectual, the spiritual, the physical, the social, or the vocational. In short, the goal of Adventist education is to develop whole persons for the whole period of existence open to them in both this world and the world to come. In that sense it transcends the possibilities of secular education, as well as many forms of Christian education, and, unfortunately, some so-called Adventist education.

One other key word in *Education*'s opening paragraph is *service* ("the joy of service in this world and . . . the higher joy of wider service in the world to come"). It should be noted that the centrality of service is not only featured in the book's first page, but also on the last, which points out: "In our life here, earthly, sin-restricted though it is, the greatest joy and the highest education are in service. And in the future state, untrammeled by the limitations of sinful humanity, it is in service that our greatest joy and our highest education will be found."[12]

That emphasis on service should come as no surprise to any reader of the Bible. Jesus more than once told His disciples that the very essence of Christian character was love for and service to others. Such characteristics, of course, are not natural human traits. "Normal" people are more concerned with their own needs and being served than they are in a life of service to others. The Christian alternative outlook and set of values does not come about naturally. Rather the Bible speaks of it as a transformation of the mind and heart (Rom. 12:2). And Paul appeals to us to let Christ's mind be our mind, pointing out that even though Christ was God, He came as a servant (Phil. 2:5–7).

In our brief overview of the key concepts of Ellen White's understanding of education, three items stand out:

- Proper education is, in essence, redemption.
- Education must aim at the preparation of the whole person and the whole period of existence possible for human beings.
- The joy of service stands at the very heart of the educative process.

Those concepts are not only central to education but also to life itself. Thus they must inform any genuine approach to Adventist educational theory and practice.

ADDITIONAL OBSERVATIONS REGARDING HUMAN NATURE

Jim Wilhoit points out that the biblical "view of human nature has no parallel in secular theories of education and is [therefore] the main obstacle to the Christian's adopting any such theory wholesale."[13] For that reason, I need to reemphasize the truth that the elements of an

Adventist approach to education must always be consciously developed in the light of human need and the human condition. We will return to the goals of Adventist education when we examine the work of the teacher. But before moving to that topic, we need to scrutinize several aspects of human nature that are of importance to Adventist education.

First is the confused status in which educators and students find themselves. On the one hand are negative perspectives on human nature. In that realm is the dictum of seventeenth-century philosopher Thomas Hobbes, who insightfully observed that human life is "solitary, poore, nasty, brutish, and short."[14] And then there are such leading lights as twentieth-century psychologist B. F. Skinner and eighteenth-century theologian Jonathan Edwards. The first claimed that people have neither freedom nor dignity,[15] while the second in his most famous sermon pictured humans as loathsome insects suspended over the pit of hell by an angry God.[16] Also, consider the view of biologist Desmond Morris, who wrote that "there are one hundred and ninety-three living species of monkeys and apes. One hundred and ninety-two of them are covered with hair." His point was that human beings comprise the exception in that they are in essence "naked apes."[17]

But are they? Holding a contrary view about human nature, the Enlightenment scholars developed the doctrine of the infinite perfectibility of humanity and the essential goodness and dignity of humans. Such modern psychologists as Carl Rogers affirmed that perspective, advocating learning theories built upon the assumption that leaving children "free" enough in a learning environment will cause their natural goodness to assert itself.[18]

So what are we to believe as educators? What is the basic nature of our students? Animal or a bit of divinity? Good or evil? The short answer is "all of the above."

Moving beyond our emotional response to Darwinism, it is difficult to deny that human beings are animals. We share much with the animal world, from structural similarities in our physical bodies to our digestive and respiratory processes. Furthermore, we participate in many of the same activities. Both people and dogs, for example, enjoy riding in automobiles, eating good food, and having their heads rubbed affectionately. Clearly, we share a great deal with our canine (and other animal) friends.

The point that needs to be emphasized, however, is not that people are animals but that they are *more* than animals. What does that mean? Jewish philosopher Abraham Heschel noted that "the animality of man we can grasp with a fair degree of clarity. The perplexity begins when we attempt to make clear what is meant by the *humanity* of man."[19]

Social theorist E. F. Schumacher wrote that humans share much with the mineral realm, since both people and minerals consist of matter; that humans have more in common with the plant world than the material realm, since both plants and people have life in addition to a mineral base; and that humans have even more yet in common with the animal world, since both people and animals have consciousness as well as life and a mineral base. But, observed Schumacher, only humans have reflective self-awareness. Animals undoubtedly think, he claimed, but humanity's uniqueness is people's self-conscious awareness of their own thinking. Schumacher pointed out that we can learn a lot about humans by studying them at the mineral, plant, and animal levels—"in fact, everything can be learned about [them] *except that which makes [them] human*."[20] For that essential insight, we noted earlier, we need to go to the Bible, in which Genesis describes essential human nature as being created in the image and likeness of the divine (Gen. 1:26, 27), although that image that has been "well-nigh obliterated" by the Fall (Gen. 3).[21]

The question that we as Christian educators need to face is how to deal with the complexities of human nature. One thing we need to recognize is that no one lives up to his or her full potential as God's image bearer. In fact, many exist at subhuman levels—at the mineral level through death, at the vegetable level through paralyzing and brain-destroying accident, or at the animal level through living primarily to satisfy their appetites and passions.

Few, of course, choose to live at the mineral or vegetable stages, but many opt for the animal level. The proverb "Every man has his price" is no idle jest. It is based upon experience and observation. Think about it for a moment. If I offered you $5 to commit a one-time-only incident or dishonest act that would never be exposed, you would probably refuse. But if I offered you $500, you might begin to think about it. By the time I got to $50,000, I would have many takers. And even the die-hards would begin to waver as the offer rose to $5 million and then $50 million.

Behavioral psychologists have discovered that animal behavior can be controlled through rewards and punishments. In other words, animals do not have freedom of choice; their needs and environment control them. Through rewards and punishments people can train an animal to do anything on command that it is capable of—including starving itself to death.

The question that has divided psychologists, educators, philosophers, and theologians is, "Can human beings be trained to do anything they are capable of?" Regarding those who live at the animal level, the answer is a definite yes. Like animals, people who operate at the level of their appetites and passions can be controlled by rewards and punishments.

Unfortunately, most people live most of their lives at the level of their animalness. This fact underlies the apparent validity of behaviorism's claim that human beings are not free and that a person's behavior can be shaped to any desired pattern if the controller has enough time and sufficient knowledge of that individual and his or her environment.

But the crucial point for educators to remember is that their students can rise above the animal level of existence. They can do so because they are uniquely related to God and because He has given them both self-awareness and the aid that Christ supplies through the Holy Spirit.

Since people bear the image of God, they can reason from cause to effect and make responsible, spiritually guided decisions. Their freedom of choice is not absolute in the sense that they are autonomous and can live without God. But it is genuine in that they can either choose Jesus Christ as Lord and live by His principles, or choose Satan as master and be subject to the law of sin and death (see Rom. 6:12–23).

The Adventist educator functions in a school full of young people in the midst of an identity crisis that impacts their lives simultaneously at several levels. One of the most important issues they face is choosing whether to live primarily at the level of their animal propensities or rise to their divine possibilities. Closely related are choices between good and evil. It doesn't help matters that educators themselves are also involved in a daily ongoing struggle over the same issues.

But the great truth of the gospel is that each person can become fully human through a personal relationship with God through Jesus Christ. That fact is a central pillar in an education whose primary purpose is helping people achieve a restored relationship with God, that sees every person as a child of God, and that seeks to help each student develop to his or her highest potential. Ellen White forcefully pointed out the infinite and eternal possibilities inherent in every person when she wrote that "higher than the highest human thought can reach is God's ideal for His children. Godliness—godlikeness—is the goal to be reached."[22] To transform that ideal from potentiality to actuality is the function of Adventist education in the home, school, and church.

A second aspect of human nature that affects Adventist education is closely related to the first: In the time that has elapsed since the Fall, the problems of the human race have not changed. Throughout history, human beings have been affected by the struggle between the forces of good and evil. Ever since the introduction of sin, there have been two basic categories of human beings—those who are still in revolt, and those who have accepted Christ as Savior. Most schools and classrooms contain students from both orientations. Sensitivity to that fact is vital to Adventist educators since they must deal daily with the complex interaction between the two types of students.

Tied to the recognition of the two types of human beings is the fact that the underlying principles of the great controversy between good and evil have remained constant despite changes in the particulars of the human predicament over time. Thus, people today face the same basic temptations and challenges that confronted Moses, David, and Paul. It is because of the unchanging nature of the human problem through both time and space (geographical location) that the Scriptures are timeless and communicate a universal message to all people. The Bible is a vital resource in education because it addresses the heart of the problem of sin and its solution—issues that all persons in every educational institution must face every day.

A third aspect of human nature that must be considered in the Adventist school is the tension between the individual and the group. On the one hand, the Christian educator must recognize and respect the individuality, uniqueness, and personal worth of each person. Throughout His life, Jesus revealed His regard for the individuality and worth of persons. His relationship both with His disciples and with the population at large contrasted with the mentality of the Pharisees, Sadducees, and even the disciples, who tended to see "others" in terms of "the herd." As it seeks to relate education to the learner, a distinctively Christian philosophy can never lose sight of the importance of human individuality.

A proper respect for individuality does not, however, negate the importance of the group. Paul, in writing to the Corinthians concerning spiritual gifts, uplifted the value of the social whole as well as the unique value of each person (1 Cor. 12:12–31). He wrote that the body (social group) will be healthy when the importance and the uniqueness of its individual members are respected. That holds true for educational institutions as well as for churches. The wholesome classroom, from that perspective, is not one of unlimited individualism, but rather one in which respect for individuality is balanced with respect for the needs of the group.

A final significant point about human nature is that the whole person is important to God. We touched upon that topic earlier in dealing with Ellen White's emphasis on wholeness in education. But we need to expand upon it. Traditional education elevated the mental dimension of students above the physical, while some modern approaches have done just the opposite. Yet others have focused on the spiritual. But whatever affects one part of a human being will eventually affect the whole. Balance among the spiritual, social, physical, and mental aspects of a person is the ideal as illustrated in the development of Jesus (Luke 2:52). Part of humanity's present dilemma is that since the Fall people have suffered from a lack of health and balance in each of these areas as well as in their interrelationships. As a result, part of the educative function of redemption is to restore people to health in each of those aspects and in their total beings. Restoration of God's image, therefore, has social, spiritual, mental, and physical ramifications, as does education. Such an understanding will have a definite impact on curriculum choices.

Christian educators, understanding the complexity of students, realize that each one is a candidate for God's kingdom and deserves the very best education that can be offered. Christian educators see beneath the veneer of outward conduct to get at the core of the human problem—sin, separation from the life and character of God. In its fullest sense, Christian education is redemption, restoration, and reconciliation. As a result, each Adventist school must seek to achieve a balance among the social, spiritual, mental, and physical aspects of each student in all of its activities and through its total program. The purpose and goal of Adventist education is the restoration of the image of God in each student and the reconciliation of students with God, their fellow students, their own selves, and the natural world. Those insights take us to the role of the Adventist teacher.

POINTS TO PONDER

- Discuss the heart of Ellen White's philosophy of education.
- In what specific ways should the Adventist view of human nature shape the church's educational system?
- In what ways does the Bible's teaching on human nature "demand" that Christian education be different from other philosophies of education?

- What are the implications of the word *whole* in Ellen White's understanding of education?
- Are people more like animals or more like God? In what ways? What are the implications of each polar position?

Notes

1. Harold H. Ditmanson, Harold V. Hong, and Warren A. Quanbeck, eds. *Christian Faith and the Liberal Arts* (Minneapolis: Augsburg, 1960), iii.

2. Gordon H. Clark, *A Christian Philosophy of Education* (Grand Rapids, MI: Eerdmans, 1946), 210.

3. This book is not the first time an Adventist philosophy of education has been formulated. See especially "A Statement of Seventh-day Adventist Educational Philosophy," developed by a group of Adventist educators for consideration at the First International Conference on the Seventh-day Adventist Philosophy of Education, convened by the General Conference Department of Education and held at Andrews University, April 7–9, 2001. That statement is published in the *Journal of Research on Christian Education* 10, special edition (Summer 2001): 347–355, and is available at the General Conference Department of Education Website. Go to http://education.gc.adventist.org; click on "publications" and choose the title of the document as listed above.

4. White, *Education*, 14–15.

5. Ibid., 15–16.

6. Ibid., 29.

7. Ibid., 30.

8. Paul Nash, *Models of Man: Explorations in the Western Educational Tradition* (New York: John Wiley and Sons, 1968); Paul Nash, Andreas M. Kazamias, and Henry J. Perkinson, *The Educated Man: Studies in the History of Educational Thought* (New York: John Wiley and Sons, 1965).

9. Allan Hart Jahsmann, *What's Lutheran in Education? Exploration into Principles and Practices* (St. Louis: Concordia, 1960), 8.

10. George R. Knight, *Philosophy and Education: An Introduction in Christian Perspective*, 4th ed. (Berrien Springs, MI: Andrews University Press, 2006), 207.

11. White, *Education*, 13.

12. Ibid., 13, 309.

13. Jim Wilhoit, *Christian Education and the Search for Meaning*, 2nd ed. (Grand Rapids, MI: Baker, 1991), 61.

14. Thomas Hobbes, *Leviathan*, ed. Richard E. Flathman and David Johnston (New York: W. W. Norton, 1997), 70.

15. B. F. Skinner, *Beyond Freedom and Dignity* (New York: Bantam, 1971).

16. Jonathan Edwards, "Sinners in the Hands of an Angry God," in *Jonathan Edwards*, ed. Clarence H. Faust and Thomas H. Johnson, rev. ed. (New York: Hill and Wang, 1962), 155–172.

17. D. Morris, *The Naked Ape*, 9.

18. Carl R. Rogers, *Freedom to Learn* (Columbus, OH: Charles E. Merrill, 1969).

19. Abraham J. Heschel, *Who Is Man?* (Stanford, CA: Stanford University Press, 1965), 3.

20. E. F. Schumacher, *A Guide for the Perplexed* (New York: Harper Colophon, 1978), 18, 20.

21. White, *Education*, 15.

22. Ibid., 18.

CHAPTER 4

The Role of the Teacher and the Aims of Adventist Education

Within the school, the teacher is the key element in educational success for he or she is the person who communicates the curriculum to the student. The best way to ensure better educational results is not improved facilities, better methods, or a more adequate curriculum, as important as those items are, but to hire and retain quality teachers. Elton Trueblood spoke to that point when he remarked that "if there is any one conclusion on which there is conspicuous agreement in our current philosophy of education it concerns the supreme importance of the good teacher. It is easy to envisage a good college with poor buildings, but it is not possible to envisage a good college with poor teachers."[1] The same, of course, holds true of elementary and secondary schools. Trueblood wrote in another connection that "it is better to have brilliant teaching in shacks than to have sloppy teaching in palaces."[2]

Some years ago, James Coleman's massive study of American schools empirically supported those observations. He found that the school factors with the greatest influence on achievement (independent of family background) were the teacher's characteristics, not facilities or curriculum.[3] Employing quality teachers is also the primary element in improving the spiritual impact of an educational program. Roger Dudley, in his study of Adventist academy students in the United States, found that *"no other factor was as strongly related to teen-age rejection of religion as was the religious sincerity of their academy teachers."*[4]

If quality teachers are the crucial factor for success in a school system that aims merely at preparing people for living and working on this earth, how much more important in an education that is preparing young people for eternity! With that thought in mind, it is of the utmost importance that Adventist parents, teachers, administrators, and school boards understand the ministry of teaching, how that ministry facilitates a school's reaching its goals, and the essential qualifications of those called to undertake the awesome task of shaping the next generation.

TEACHING IS A FORM OF MINISTRY

Since education and redemption are one,[5] Adventist teaching by definition is a form of Christian ministry and a pastoral function. The New Testament clearly defines teaching as a divine calling (Rom. 12:6–8; 1 Cor. 12:28; Eph. 4:11). Furthermore, the Scriptures do not separate the functions of teaching and pastoring. On the contrary, Paul wrote to Timothy that a bishop (pastor) must be "an apt teacher" (1 Tim. 3:2). In writing to the Ephesians that "some should be apostles, some prophets, some evangelists, some pastors and teachers" (Eph. 4:11), Paul used a Greek construction that indicates that the same person holds both the office of pastor and teacher. F. F. Bruce, in commenting on this passage, has remarked that "the two terms 'pastors (shepherds) and teachers' denote one and the same class of men."[6] By contrast, Scripture lists the other gifts separately. The significance of this point is that we cannot divide these two gifts if they are to remain functional. Pastors must not only care for the souls of their flock, but also teach by precept and example both to individuals and the corporate body of the church. Teachers, likewise, must not merely transmit truth but also commit themselves to caring for the individuals under their tutelage. Thus, Christian teachers function in a pastoral role to their students.

The major difference between the roles of pastors and teachers in our day has to do with the current division of labor. In twenty-first-century society, the Christian teacher may be seen as one who pastors in a school context, while the pastor is one who teaches in the larger religious community. It is important to remember that their function is essentially the same, even though by today's definitions they have charge of different divisions of the Lord's vineyard.

Teaching young people is not only a pastoral function but also one of the most effective forms of ministry, since it reaches the entire population while at its most impressionable age. Reformer Martin Luther recognized that fact when he wrote that "if I had to give up preaching and my other duties, there is no office I would rather have than that of school-teacher. For I know that next to the [pastoral] ministry it is the most useful, greatest, and best; and I am not sure which of the two is to be preferred. For it is hard to make old dogs docile and old rogues pious, yet that is what the ministry works at, and must work at, in great part, in vain; but young trees . . . are more easily bent and trained. Therefore let it be considered one of the highest virtues on earth faithfully to train the children of others, which duty but very few parents attend to themselves."[7]

The clearest and fullest integration of the gift of teacher-pastor appeared in the ministry of Christ. One of the terms by which people most addressed Him was "Master." The actual meaning of the Greek word is "Teacher." Christ may be seen as the best example of teaching in terms of both methodology and meaningful interpersonal relationships. A study of the Gospels from the perspective of Christ as teacher will contribute a great deal to our understanding of ideal Christian instruction.

We will examine Christ's teaching methodology in a subsequent chapter. But here we will study the relationship aspect of His teaching ministry, an especially important topic since good relationships stand at the very center of successful teaching. Several statements from Ellen White offer insight into this topic.

Part of the reason for the success of Christ's ministry was that people knew that He really cared. For example, we read that "in His work as a public teacher, Christ never lost sight of the children. . . . His presence never repelled them. His large heart of love could comprehend their trials and necessities, and find happiness in their simple joys; and he took them in His arms and blessed them."[8] Children are quite perceptive. They can tell after talking to an adult whether that person is just listening to their small joys and concerns to be polite or feels genuine interest—if he or she really cares. How many times have we as parents or teachers listened to our children, nodded our heads, and then sent them off to play without having the slightest idea what they were trying to communicate? An excellent way to alienate children is to let them feel that grown-ups are more concerned with "important" adult thoughts than with their well-being. Ellen White has suggested that even if teachers have limited literary qualifications, if they really care for their students, realize the magnitude of their task, and have a willingness to improve, they will succeed.[9] At the very heart of Christ's teaching ministry was the caring relationship.

That relationship in His case exuded a spirit of confidence regarding the possibilities of each life. Thus, even though "Christ was a faithful reprover," in "every human being, however fallen, He beheld a son of God, one who might be restored to the privilege of his divine relationship. . . . Looking upon men in their suffering and degradation, Christ perceived ground for hope where appeared only despair and ruin. Wherever there existed a sense of need, there He saw opportunity for uplifting. Souls tempted, defeated, feeling themselves lost, ready to perish, He met, not with denunciation, but with blessing. . . .

"In every human being He discerned infinite possibilities. He saw men as they might be, transfigured by His grace. . . . Looking upon them with hope, He inspired hope. Meeting them with confidence, He inspired trust. Revealing in Himself man's true ideal, He awakened, for its attainment, both desire and faith. In His presence souls despised and fallen realized that they still were men, and they longed to prove themselves worthy of His regard. In many a heart that seemed dead to all things holy, were awakened new impulses. To many a despairing one there opened the possibility of a new life. Christ bound men to His heart by the ties of love and devotion."[10]

That quotation highlights the very spirit of Christ's teaching ministry that made Him such a force for good in the lives of those He taught. The statement itself contains the ultimate challenge for teachers, parents, and everyone else who works with human beings. To see infinite possibilities in every person, to see hope in the hopeless, takes an infusion of God's grace. But it is the key to good teaching. The alternative is to look upon people with hopelessness and thereby inspire hopelessness.

Psychologist Arthur Combs cites several research studies that indicate that good teachers can be clearly distinguished from poor ones on the basis of what they believe about people.[11] In a similar vein, William Glasser, the psychiatrist who developed "reality therapy," believes that failures in both school and life find their roots in two related problems—the failure to love and the failure to achieve self-worth.[12] We develop our self-worth from our perceptions of what others think of us. When parents and teachers constantly give messages that children are stupid, delinquent, and hopeless, they are shaping these young people's sense of self-worth, which the youth will act out in daily living.

Fortunately, the self-fulfilling prophecy also works in the positive direction. Earl Pullias and James Young note that "when people are asked to describe the teacher that did the most for them, again and again they mention a teacher, often the only one in their experience, who believed in them, who saw their special talents, not only what they were but even more what they wanted to be and could be. And they began to learn not only in the area of their special interest but in many others." As such, a teacher is an inspirer of vision.[13]

On the other hand, Christ's ability to see the potential in each person did not entail a blindness to human limitations. Within the biblical framework, no one has every talent, even though each has some. At times students need definite guidance into areas where their personalities and natural gifts will make them most effective. So it was in Christ's ministry. He knew the special needs and potentials of Peter, John, and Andrew and guided them accordingly.

While the caring relationship was central to Christ's teaching ministry, that relationship was carefully balanced in daily practice. Thus Ellen White writes that "He showed consistency without obstinacy, benevolence without weakness, tenderness and sympathy without sentimentalism. He was highly social, yet He possessed a reserve that discouraged any familiarity. His temperance never led to bigotry or austerity. He was not conformed to the world, yet He was attentive to the wants of the least among men."[14]

Adventist teachers and others concerned with the church's education system will gain much through a study of Christ as the Master Teacher. Such a study will also put them in direct contact with the aims and goals of Christian education.

THE PRIMARY AIM OF EDUCATION AND THE ADVENTIST TEACHER AS AN AGENT OF REDEMPTION

We have already noted that from both the Bible and Ellen White's perspective the greatest human need is to get into a right relationship with God. Said in another way, human lostness provides the purpose of Christian education. The greatest human need is to become unlost. Thus Jesus claimed that He came "to seek and to save that which was lost" (Luke 19:10, KJV). Such seeking and saving is the theme of the Bible from Genesis to Revelation.

Luke 15, which records the parables of the lost sheep, the lost coin, and the lost son, is especially pertinent as we think about the role of the Christian teacher. The teacher, from the perspective of that chapter, is someone who seeks out and attempts to help those lost and caught in the web of sin, whether they are like (1) the sheep (those who know they are lost but do not know how to get home); (2) the coin and older son (those who do not have enough spiritual sense to realize their own lostness); or (3) the younger son (those who know they are lost and know how to get home, but do not want to return until their rebellion has run its course). Lostness has many varieties, all of which are exhibited in each school and classroom. But both rebels and Pharisees and all the other types of human beings have one common need—to get unlost. Thus, it is little wonder that Christ identified the core of His mission as seeking and saving the lost (Luke 19:10).

To those passages may be added Jesus's experience with the ungrateful and inhospitable Samaritans when they refused to provide Him with a place to stay because they perceived He was on His way to Jerusalem. On that occasion, James and John were incensed with the ingratitude of the Samaritans and sought Jesus's permission to call down fire from heaven to destroy them. Jesus responded that "the Son of man is not come to destroy men's lives, but to save them" (Luke 9:51–56, KJV).

The primary goal of Christ's life and of Christian education can also be found in the keynote verse of the Gospel of Matthew, which predicted that Mary would bear a son who would "save his people from their sins" (Matt. 1:21). The same thought is brought out by John's Gospel, which claims that "God so loved the world that he gave his only Son, that whosoever believes in him should not perish but have eternal life. For God sent the Son into the world, not to condemn the world, but that the world might be saved through him" (John 3:16, 17).

Adventist teachers are God's agents in the plan of redemption and reconciliation. Like Christ, their primary function is "to seek and to save the lost" (Luke 19:10). They must be willing to work in the spirit of Christ, so that their students can be brought into harmony with God through the sacrifice of Jesus and be restored to God's image.

Teaching is much more than transmitting information and filling students' heads with knowledge. It is more than preparing them for the world of work. The primary function of the Christian teacher is to relate to the Master Teacher in such a way that he or she becomes God's agent in the redemptive plan.

Edwin Rian caught that point when he noted that most writers in educational philosophy, regardless of their philosophical and religious perspectives, "agree on considering the problem of 'sin and death,' which is the problem of man, according to Pauline and Reformed Protestant theology, as irrelevant to the questions of the aims and process of education." Such a position, he indicated, cannot help producing "miseducation and frustration for the individual and for the community." From the perspective of humanity's predicament, Rian uplifted *"education as conversion."*[15] Herbert Welch, president of Ohio Wesleyan University early in the twentieth century, made the same point when he claimed that "to win its students from sin to righteousness is . . . the highest achievement of a Christian college."[16]

Christian education is the only education that can meet humanity's deepest needs, because only Christian educators understand the core of the human problem. The redemptive aim of Christian education is what makes it Christian. The primary aim of Christian education in the school, the home, and the church is to lead people into a saving relationship with Jesus Christ. That restored relationship heals the principal alienation in Genesis 3—that between humans and God. And the healing of the God/human relationship sets the stage for the removal of humanity's other basic alienations. Thus education is a part of God's great plan of redemption or atonement. Its role is to help bring people back to at oneness with God, other people, one's own self, and the natural world. The whole message of the Bible points forward to the day when the work of restoration will be complete and the Edenic condition will be restored in the realm of nature because of the healing of humanity's manifold lostness (Isa. 11:6–9; 35; Rev. 21, 22).

The essence of the Fall was human beings' decision to place themselves rather than God at the center of their lives. Redemption reinstates God as the focal point of personal existence. It is a dynamic experience called by many names, including conversion and new birth. The Bible also refers to it as the obtaining of a new heart and mind. Paul vividly described the experience when he claimed that the Christian is one who has had his or her entire way of thinking and living transformed (Rom. 12:2). The Greek word he used for transformation is *metamorphosis*, the term we use in English to indicate the change that takes place when a caterpillar becomes a butterfly. It is a radical change that involves a discontinuity with the past and a new beginning. Carlyle B. Haynes caught the central nature of the experience when he wrote that "the Christian life is not any modification of the old life; it is not any qualification of it, any development of it, not any progression of it, any culture or refinement or education of it. It is not built on the old life at all. It does not grow from it. It is entirely another life—a new life altogether. It is the actual life of Jesus Christ Himself in my flesh."[17]

The student's greatest need, then, is for a spiritual rebirth that places God at the center of daily existence. Paul noted that such renewal is a daily experience (1 Cor. 15:31), and Jesus taught that the Holy Spirit accomplishes the transformation (John 3:5, 6). Christian education is thus impossible without the dynamic power of the Holy Spirit.

Ellen White wrote that the "all-important thing" in education "should be the conversion of . . . students, that they may have a new heart and life. The object of the Great Teacher is the restoration of the image of God in the soul, and every teacher in our schools should work in harmony with this purpose."[18] Adventist education can build upon the foundation of the new birth experience to achieve its other aims and purposes. But if it fails at this foundational and primary point, it has failed entirely.

SOME SECONDARY AIMS OF ADVENTIST EDUCATION

The healing of humanity's alienation from God sets the stage for treating its other basic alienations and thereby helps to define the secondary purposes of education. We have repeatedly noted that education is a part of God's great plan of redemption or atonement; that education's role is to help bring people back to at-one-ness with God, their fellow humans, their own selves, and the natural world. Within that context, the focal point of Christian teaching is the healing of broken relationships between individuals and God. This, in turn, prepares the way for Christian education to accomplish its secondary purposes, such as character development, the acquisition of knowledge, job preparation, and the nurturing of students socially, emotionally, and physically.

Character development is certainly a major goal of Adventist education. Ellen White noted that character determines destiny for both this life and the one to come and that "character building is the most important work ever entrusted to human beings."[19] C. B. Eavey related character development to the fundamental purpose of education when he stated that "the foundational aim in Christian education is the bringing of the individual to Christ for salvation. Before a man of God can be perfected, there must be a man of God to perfect; without the new birth there is no man of God."[20] In other words, true character can develop only in the born-again Christian. When we equate the primary objective of Christian education—to bring students into relationship with Christ—with such theological concepts as conversion, new birth, and justification, it follows that character development, as a secondary aim, must be synonymous with sanctification and Christian growth in grace.

Such an equation is exactly what we find in the writings of Ellen White. "The great work of parents and teachers," she penned, "is character building—seeking to restore the image of Christ in those placed under their care. A knowledge of the sciences sinks into insignificance beside this great aim; but all true education may be made to help in the development of a righteous character. The formation of character is the work of a lifetime, and it is for eternity."[21]

Character development and sanctification are essentially two names for the same process. Educators and theologians have, unfortunately, developed different vocabularies to describe the same process. At this point, it is important to remember that the concept of Christian character development is antithetical to the humanistic view, which implies merely a refinement of the natural, unrenewed person. Christian character development never occurs outside the conversion experience or apart from Christ and the agency of the Holy Spirit (John 15:1–17; Phil. 2:12, 13). Only the dynamic power of the Holy Spirit can develop the image of God in the individual and reproduce the fruit of the Spirit—love, joy, peace, patience, kindness, goodness, faithfulness, gentleness, and self-control—in the life of each student (Gal. 5:22–24). Hans LaRondelle has indicated that at least part of the restoration process occurs as we behold the "attractive loveliness of Christ's character." Through that experience we assimilate His image.[22] Thus it is imperative that every aspect of Adventist education—the character of the teacher, the curriculum, the methods of discipline, and every other aspect—reflects Christ.

Jesus Christ is the beginning, the middle, and the end of Adventist education. The Holy Spirit seeks to implant the likeness of Christ's character in each of us as educators and in our children and students. The Spirit uses parents, teachers, and other educators as agents or mediators of salvation. But each person must continuously surrender the will to God's infilling power and then follow the directions of the Holy Spirit in his or her life. Character development is an act of God's grace just as much as justification. Because of its vital role, the science of character development should form a central pillar in the preparation of teachers, parents, and others in positions of educational influence.

Adventist education obviously has other, secondary, goals such as the acquisition of knowledge and preparation for the world of work, but such goals sink into "insignificance" when compared to the redemptive work of education, which relates to conversion and character development.[23] After all, "what is a man profited, if he shall gain the whole world, and lose his own soul?" (Matt. 16:26, KJV).

Beyond character development, another secondary goal of Christian education is the development of a Christian mind. While that task does involve the transmission of information, it is far broader than that. It means helping students gain a way of viewing reality and organizing knowledge within the framework of the Christian worldview. Gene Garrick pointed out the secondary importance of knowledge acquisition when he wrote that "there can be no truly Christian mind without the new birth since spiritual truth is apprehended and applied spiritually (1 Cor. 2:1–16)."[24]

We will return to the discussion of developing the Christian mind at greater length in the chapter on curriculum. But before leaving the topic, it is important to point out that a Christian never views gaining knowledge—even biblical or Christian knowledge—as an end in itself. In acquiring knowledge and in developing a Christian mind, Christian teachers must never lose sight of their ultimate goal for their students: more effective service to both God and their fellow beings. Thus knowledge, from a Christian perspective, is instrumental rather than an end in itself.

Another secondary aim of Adventist education is to maximize physical and emotional health. Ellen White wrote that "since the mind and the soul find expression through the body, both mental and spiritual vigor are in great degree dependent upon physical strength and activity; whatever promotes physical health, promotes the development of a strong mind and a well-balanced character. Without health no one can as distinctly understand or as completely fulfill his obligations to himself, to his fellow beings, or to his Creator. Therefore the health should be as faithfully guarded as the character. A knowledge of physiology and hygiene should be the basis of all educational effort."[25]

Because human beings are not merely spiritual, or mental, or physical machines but wholistic creations in which imbalance in one aspect of their nature affects the whole, it is crucial that the educational system also promotes emotional health. After all, angry, depressed individuals cannot relate to either God or their fellow human beings in a functional manner. Since the Fall fractured God's image spiritually, socially, mentally, and physically, education must aim at restoring health and wholeness in each of those areas and in their interrelationship with one another.

A final secondary aim of Adventist education is to prepare students for the world of work, a topic on which Ellen White had a great deal to say. From her perspective, useful labor is a blessing to both the individual and the community and "a part of God's great plan for our recovery from the Fall."[26] Career preparation, however, like every other aspect of the Christian life, cannot be separated from the issues of the new birth, character development, the development of a Christian mind, the achievement of physical and mental well-being, and the development of a sense of social responsibility. The Christian life is a unit, and each aspect of it interacts with the others and the total person. Thus, Adventist teachers will encourage their students to view even so-called secular occupations within the context of an individual's wider vocation as a servant of God and humankind. That idea brings us to the ultimate and final goal of Adventist education.

THE ULTIMATE AIM OF ADVENTIST EDUCATION

The life of Jesus was one of service for humanity. He came to our planet to give Himself for the betterment of others. Thus, His followers have the same function, and the ultimate end (i.e., final outcome) of educa-tion is to prepare students for that task. Along that line, Herbert Welch concluded that "education for its own sake is as bad as art for art's sake; but culture held in trust to empower one better to serve one's fellow men, the wise for the ignorant, the strong for the weak" is education's highest aim. "The Christian character," he postulated, "which does not find expression in service is scarcely worthy of the name."[27]

Ellen White agreed. Beginning and ending her classic *Education* with the "joy" of service, she considered it the "highest education."[28] "The true teacher," she noted, "is not satisfied with second-rate work. He is not satisfied with directing his students to a standard lower than the highest which it is possible for them to attain. He cannot be con-tent with imparting to them only technical knowledge, with making them merely clever accountants, skillful artisans, successful trades-men. It is his ambition to inspire them with principles of truth, obedi-ence, honor, integrity, and purity—principles that will make them a positive force for the stability and uplifting of society. He desires them, above all else, to learn life's great lesson of unselfish service."[29]

Figure 2 indicates that conversion, character development, acquiring a mature Christian mind and good health, and occupational preparation are not ends in themselves. Each is, instead, an essential element in a person's preparation for service to humanity as part of God's plan to heal the alienation between people that developed at the

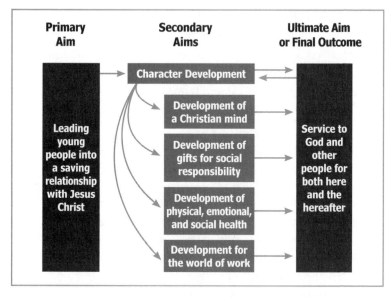

Primary Aim	Secondary Aims	Ultimate Aim or Final Outcome

Character Development

Leading young people into a saving relationship with Jesus Christ

Development of a Christian mind

Development of gifts for social responsibility

Development of physical, emotional, and social health

Development for the world of work

Service to God and other people for both here and the hereafter

FIGURE 2.   Purposes of Christian Education That Inform Teaching

Fall. The essence of Christian love and of the Christlike character is service to others.

Teachers should help their students realize that most people have gotten their educational priorities backward. We hear the following sentiments: "Society owes me a good living because of all the years I spent getting an education." "I deserve the benefits of the good life because of what I have accomplished." Even those who claim to be Christians often hold—or at least imply—such sentiments. Unfortunately, these ideas represent the antithesis of the ultimate aim of Christianity.

It is morally wrong for people to use the benefits of society's gift of education for self-aggrandizement. George S. Counts wrote from a humanistic perspective that "at every turn the social obligation which the advantages of a college education impose must be stressed: too often have we preached the monetary value of a college education; too widely have we bred the conviction that the training is advantageous because it enables the individual to get ahead; too insidiously have we spread the doctrine that the college opens up avenues to the exploitation of less capable men. Higher education involves higher responsibility . . . ; this cardinal truth must be impressed upon every recipient of its advantages. In season and out of season, social service, and not individual advancement, must be the motif of college training."[30] If Counts from his secular perspective saw that fact so clearly, then the committed Christian should recognize it even more distinctly.

The message of the parable of the talents is that the greater a person's natural endowments and his or her opportunities for their development, the more responsibility he or she has to represent Christ in faithful service to those with mental, spiritual, social, emotional, or physical needs (Matt. 25:14–30).

The Christian teacher has the responsibility not only to teach the ideal of service, but also to model it. Thus, a major task of Christian education is to "help students unwrap their God-given gifts" so that they can find their place in service to others.[31]

In conclusion, it should be emphasized that Christian service is a response to God's love rather than an altruistic humanitarianism that still allows people to congratulate themselves for their personal goodness and sacrifice. The Christian's gratitude to God for salvation inspires him or her to become a channel of God's love by participating in His ministry of reconciliation.

In one sense, as we note in Figure 2, character development lays the foundation for service. But such service also helps to develop character (thus the two-way arrow between character development and service). As a result, the two work in tandem, each contributing to the other. It is a truism that character development cannot occur without service, but it is equally true that character leads to service.

Teachers should seek to instill in their students the conviction that Christian service is not something that begins after graduation or when they are older. Rather, it is an integral part of a Christian's life from the time of conversion. Teachers in the church, home, and school need to provide their students with opportunities for serving others both inside and outside their religious communities. In short, a crucial function of Christian teaching is to help students not only internalize God's love but also to externalize it. Teachers, as agents of redemption, need to help their students discover their personal roles in God's plan of reconciliation and restoration.

QUALIFICATIONS OF THE ADVENTIST TEACHER

Because of the centrality of the teacher to the educational process, it is absolutely essential that teachers be in harmony with the philosophy and goals of the schools for which they teach. With that in mind, Frank Gaebelein wrote that there can be "no Christian education without Christian teachers."[32] It is just as true that *there can be no Adventist education without Adventist teachers.* That is true because of the distinctive doctrinal understandings and apocalyptic mission that set Adventism apart from other Christian perspectives and must inform the content of Adventist education.

The selection of qualified teachers and consecrated school employees is of crucial importance, given their powerful role in the educational process. Along that line, Ellen White stressed that "in selecting teachers we should use every precaution, knowing that this is as solemn a matter as the selecting of persons for the ministry.... The very best talent that can be secured is needed to educate and mold the minds of the young and to carry on successfully the many lines of work that will need to be done by the teacher in our ... schools."[33] No one wants to hire underqualified physicians, lawyers, or airplane pilots, even if they are cheaper. Why should there be a blind spot in hiring qualified teachers—individuals who work with the most valuable entities on earth, the future generation?

First in importance among the qualifications is the spiritual. That is true because the essence of the human problem is sin or a spiritual disorientation from God. It is sin, as we noted earlier, that is at the root of all the other alienations and disorientations that are so destructive both to individuals and societies. The Bible teaches that humanity in its natural condition is suffering from a form of spiritual death (Gen. 3), and that the greatest need of people is a spiritual rebirth

(John 3:3, 5). C. B. Eavey has written that "only one who has been made a new creature in Christ can mediate to others God's grace or nurture others in that grace." As a result, those who minister in Christian education "must have in themselves the life of Christ and be possessed by the Spirit of God. Christian education is no matter of mere human activity but one of individuals meeting God in Christ."[34]

Ellen White expands upon that idea when she writes that "it is only life that can beget life. He alone has life who is connected with the Source of life, and only such can be a channel of life. In order that the teacher may accomplish the object of his work, he should be a living embodiment of truth, a living channel through which wisdom and life may flow. A pure life, the result of sound principles and right habits, should therefore be regarded as his most essential qualification."[35]

Thus, qualification number one for Adventist teachers is that they have a personal saving relationship with Jesus. If their spiritual life is in harmony with God's revealed will, they will have a reverence for the sacred, and their daily example will be one from which their students can profit.

A second qualification relates to their mental capabilities and development. "While right principles and correct habits are of first importance among the qualifications of the teacher," Ellen White wrote, "it is indispensable that he should have a thorough knowledge of the sciences. With uprightness of character, high literary acquirements should be combined."[36]

But Adventist teachers must not only be well versed in the general knowledge of their culture. They must also have a grasp of the truths of Scripture and be able to communicate the subjects they teach in the context of the Christian and Adventist worldview. They should be individuals who can lead their students beyond the narrow realm of their field of study by relating each course to the ultimate meaning of human existence.

A third area of development underlying the qualification of Adventist teachers is the social. The social relationships of Christ with His pupils in the Gospels make an interesting and profitable study. He did not seek to isolate Himself from those He was teaching. Rather, He mixed with them and engaged in their social events.

Ellen White has written that "the true teacher can impart to his pupils few gifts so valuable as the gift of his own companionship. . . . To strengthen the tie of sympathy between teacher and student there are few means that count so much as pleasant association together outside the schoolroom."[37] On another occasion, she suggested that if teachers "would gather the children close to them, and show that they love them, and would manifest an interest in all their efforts, and even in their sports, sometimes even being a child among children, they would make the children very happy, and would gain their love and win their confidence. And the children would sooner respect and love . . . [their] authority."[38] To a large extent, the relationship between teacher and student outside the classroom colors and conditions the one inside it.

A fourth sphere of teacher qualification is good physical, mental, and emotional health. Without balanced health, a teacher will find it well-nigh impossible to maintain a sunny disposition and an even temper that reflect the image of Christ.

Christian teachers must strive for the continual improvement of their personal qualifications. That is the same as the goal that they seek for their students—a restoration of the image of God physically, mentally, spiritually, and socially. That balance, as it is found in the life of Christ, will form the basis for their professional activity. Because teaching is the art of loving God's children, Adventist teachers should have a desire to let God make them the most effective lovers possible.

Said in another way, an overall qualification of Christian teachers is to be a good model or example of what they want their students to be in every aspect of their lives. It is almost impossible to overestimate the power of a teacher as an example for either good or evil. Pullias and Young note that "being an example arises out of the very nature of teaching" and that "being a model is a part of teaching that no teacher can escape."[39] Ellen White highlights the facts that "the teacher should be himself what he wishes his students to become" and that "in His life, Christ's words had perfect illustration and support. . . . It was this that gave His teaching . . . power."[40]

What has been said about the qualifications of teachers also applies to other employees in an Adventist school. They, too, make a significant impact on students and thus need to be not only spiritual leaders but also healthy and balanced in every way. Teachers are only one part of an effective, integrated educational team.

Chapters 3 and 4 have examined, from the perspective of a biblical philosophy, the nature of the student, the role of the teacher, and the aims of Adventist education. Chapters 5–7 will develop an Adventist approach to curriculum, explore the implications of a biblical perspective for teaching methodology, and discuss the social role of Adventist education in the context of the great controversy between good and evil.

POINTS TO PONDER

- In what ways is Christian teaching a form of ministry?
- How does the ministry function affect a teacher's aims?
- In what ways does the view of teaching as ministry enrich our understanding of the importance of Adventist education?
- In your own words, describe the purpose(s) of Adventist education.
- What are the implications of that/those purpose(s) for you personally as a teacher?

Notes

1. David Elton Trueblood, *The Idea of a College* (New York: Harper and Brothers, 1959), 33.

2. David Elton Trueblood, "The Marks of a Christian College," in *Toward a Christian Philosophy of Higher Education*, ed. John Paul von Grueningen (Philadelphia: Westminster, 1957), 168.

3. James S. Coleman et al., *Equality of Educational Opportunity* (Washington, DC: U. S. Department of Health, Education, and Welfare, 1966).

4. Roger L. Dudley, *Why Teenagers Reject Religion and What to Do About It*

(Washington, DC: Review and Herald, 1978), 80.

5. White, *Education*, 16, 30.

6. F. F. Bruce, *The Epistle to the Ephesians* (Westwood, NJ: Fleming H. Revell, 1961), 85.

7. Martin Luther, "Sermon on the Duty of Sending Children to School," in *Luther on Education*, ed. F. V. N. Painter (Philadelphia: Lutheran Publication Society, 1889), 264.

8. White, *Counsels to Parents, Teachers, and Students*, 179.

9. White, *Education*, 279.

10. Ibid., 79–80.

11. Arthur W. Combs, *Myths in Education: Beliefs That Hinder Progress and Their Alternatives* (Boston: Allyn and Bacon, 1979), 196–197.

12. William Glasser, *Schools Without Failure* (New York: Harper and Row, 1975), 14. For more on Glasser, see Jim Roy, *Soul Shapers: A Better Plan for Parents and Educators* (Hagerstown, MD: Review and Herald, 2005).

13. Earl V. Pullias and James D. Young, *A Teacher Is Many Things*, 2nd ed. (Bloomington, IN: Indiana University Press, 1977), 128.

14. White, *Counsels to Parents, Teachers, and Students,* 262.

15. Edwin H. Rian, "The Need: A World View," in *Toward a Christian Philosophy of Higher Education*, ed. John Paul von Grueningen (Philadelphia: Westminster, 1957), 30–31.

16. Herbert Welch, "The Ideals and Aims of the Christian College," in *The Christian College*, ed. Herbert Welch, Henry Churchill King, and Thomas Nicholson (New York: Methodist Book Concern, 1916), 21.

17. Carlyle B. Haynes, *Righteousness in Christ: A Preacher's Personal Experience* (Takoma Park, MD: General Conference Ministerial Association, [c. 1926]), 9–10.

18. White, *Fundamentals of Christian Education*, 436.

19. White, *Education*, 109, 225.

20. C. B. Eavey, "Aims and Objectives of Christian Education," in *An Introduction to Evangelical Christian Education*, ed. J. Edward Hakes (Chicago: Moody, 1964), 62.

21. White, *Counsels to Parents, Teachers, and Students*, 61.

22. Hans K. LaRondelle, *Christ Our Salvation: What God Does for Us and in Us* (Mountain View, CA: Pacific Press, 1980), 81–82.

23. White, *Counsels to Parents, Teachers, and Students*, 49, 61; White, *Fundamentals of Christian Education*, 27.

24. Gene Garrick, "Developing Educational Objectives for the Christian School," in *The Philosophy of Christian School Education*, ed. Paul A. Kienel, 2nd ed. (Whittier, CA: Association of Christian Schools International, 1978), 73.

25. White, *Education*, 195.

26. Ibid., 214.

27. Welch, "The Ideals and Aims of the Christian College," 23-22.

28. White, *Education*, 13, 309.

29. Ibid., 29-30.

30. J. Crosby Chapman and George S. Counts, *Principles of Education* (Boston: Houghton Mifflin, 1924), 498.

31. Gloria Goris Stronks and Doug Blomberg, eds., *A Vision with a Task: Christian Schooling for Responsive Discipleship* (Grand Rapids, MI: Baker, 1993), 25.

32. Frank E. Gaebelein, *The Pattern of God's Truth: Problems of Integration in Christian Education* (Chicago: Moody, 1968), 35.

33. White, *Testimonies for the Church*, vol. 6, 200; cf. White, *Counsels to Parents, Teachers, and Students*, 150-151.

34. Eavey, "Aims and Objectives of Christian Education," 61.

35. White, *Counsels to Parents, Teachers, and Students*, 31.

36. Ibid., 199.

37. White, *Education*, 212; cf. White, *Counsels to Parents, Teachers, and Students*, 502; White, *Fundamentals of Christian Education*, 116.

38. White, *Fundamentals of Christian Education*, 18-19.

39. Pullias and Young, *A Teacher Is Many Things*, 68.

40. White, *Counsels to Parents, Teachers, and Students*, 65; White, *Education*, 78-79.

CHAPTER 5

Curriculum Considerations

The term *curriculum* comes from the Latin word *currere*, which means to run a race." In a general sense it represents "all the courses and experiences at an institution."[1] One author defines it as "a road map in broad strokes that points individuals in the direction of Christian maturing."[2]

But, we need ask, what should be included in the map? And on what basis should decisions be made? Those questions bring us to the issue of what knowledge is of most worth.

WHAT KNOWLEDGE IS OF MOST WORTH?

One of the most enlightening and coherent essays ever published on the relationship of philosophic beliefs to the content of the curriculum was developed by Herbert Spencer (a leading social Darwinist) in 1854. "What Knowledge Is of Most Worth?" was both the title and the central question of the essay. To Spencer, this was the "question of questions" in the realm of education. "Before there can be a rational *curriculum*," he argued, "we must settle which things it most concerns us to know; . . . we must determine the relative value of knowledges."[3]

Spencer, in seeking to answer his question, classified human activity in a hierarchical order based on importance. He chose the following stratification, in terms of descending consequence: (1) those activities relating directly to self-preservation, (2) those activities that indirectly minister to self-preservation, (3) those activities having to do with the rearing of offspring, (4) those activities pertaining to political and social relations, (5) those activities that relate to the leisure part of life and are devoted to the tastes and appetites.[4]

His essay then proceeded to analyze human affairs from a naturalistic-evolutionary perspective, and eventually provided an unequivocal reply to his leading question: "What knowledge is of most worth?—the uniform reply is—Science. This is the verdict on all the counts." Spencer's explanation of his answer related Science (broadly conceived to include the social and practical sciences, as well as the physical and life sciences) to his five-point hierarchy of life's most important activities. His answer was built upon the principle that whichever activities occupy the peripheral aspects of life should also occupy marginal places in the curriculum, while those activities that are most important in life should be given the most important place in the course of studies.[5]

Christians will of necessity reject Spencer's conclusions, which are built upon a naturalistic metaphysics and epistemology, but they must not miss the larger issue underlying his argument. It is crucial that Adventists understand the rationale for the curriculum in their institutions of learning. Mark Van Doren noted that "the college is meaningless without a curriculum, but it is more so when it has one that is meaningless."[6]

The Adventist educator must, with Spencer, settle the issue of "which things it most concerns us to know." The answer to that question, as Spencer noted, leads directly to an understanding of the relative values of various kinds of knowledge in the curriculum. Adventist educators can study Spencer's essay and the methodology included therein and gain substantial insights into the important task of curriculum development in the context of their distinctive worldview.

Authentic and viable curricula must be developed out of, and must be consistent with, a school's metaphysical, epistemological, and axiological bases. It is therefore a foundational truth that different philosophic approaches will emphasize different curricula. One implication of that fact is that the curriculum of Adventist schools will not be a readjustment or an adaptation of the secular curriculum of the larger society. Biblical Christianity is unique. Therefore, the curricular stance of Adventist education will be unique.

Another major issue in curriculum development is to discover the pattern that holds the curriculum together. Alfred North Whitehead claimed that curricular programs generally suffer from the lack of an integrating principle. "Instead of this single unity, we offer children—Algebra, from which nothing follows; Geometry, from which nothing follows; Science, from which nothing follows; History, from which nothing follows; a Couple of Languages, never mastered; and lastly, most dreary of all, Literature, represented by plays of Shakespeare, with philological notes and short analyses of plot and character to be in substance committed to memory. Can such a list be said to represent Life, as it is known in the midst of the living of it? The best that can be said of it is that it is a rapid table of contents which a deity might run over in his mind while he was thinking of creating a world, and has not yet determined how to put it together."[7]

However, the crux of the problem has not been ignorance of the need for some overall pattern in which to fit together the various subjects of the curriculum in such a way that they make sense, but to discover such a pattern. We live in a world that has so fragmented knowledge that it is difficult to see how our various realms of expertise relate to the whole. It is in this context that C. P. Snow's "Two Cultures"—with its discussion of the great gulf between the humanities and the sciences—takes on particular significance and meaning.[8]

Our world is one in which subject-area scholars have too often lost the ability to communicate with one another because they fail to see the significance of their subject matter in relation to the big picture. To complicate matters, we find existentialists and postmodernists denying external meaning, and analytic philosophers suggesting that since we can't discover meaning, we should focus on defining our words and refining our syntax.

The search for meaning in the total educational experience has been a major quest for more than a century. Some have defined the integrating center as the unity of the classics, while others have viewed it in terms of the needs of society, vocationalism, or science. None of those approaches, however, has been broad enough, and their claims have usually been divisive rather than unifying. We seem to live in a schizophrenic world in which many claim that there is no external meaning, while others base their scientific research on postulates that point to an overall meaning. Modern secular people have thrown out Christianity as a unifying force and have tended to concentrate on the details of their knowledge rather than on the whole. As a result, intellectual fragmentation continues to be a large problem as human beings seek to determine what knowledge is of most worth.

For Adventist educators, the problem is quite different. They know what knowledge is of most worth, because they understand humanity's greatest needs. They know that the Bible is a cosmic revelation that transcends the limited realm of humanity, and that it not only reveals the human condition but also the remedy for that condition. They further realize that all subject matter becomes meaningful when seen in the light of the Bible and its Great Controversy struggle between good and evil. The problem for Adventist educators has not been to *find* the pattern of knowledge in relation to its center, but rather to *apply* what they know.

All too often the curriculum of Christian schools, including Adventist institutions, has been "a patchwork of naturalistic ideas mixed with Biblical truth." That has led, Frank Gaebelein claims, to a form of "scholastic schizophrenia in which a highly orthodox theology coexists uneasily with a teaching of non-religious subjects that differs little from that in secular institutions."[9] The challenge confronting the curriculum developer in an Adventist school is to move beyond a curricular view focused on the bits and pieces, and to find a way to clearly and purposefully integrate the details of knowledge into the biblical framework. That task brings us to the unity of truth.

THE UNITY OF TRUTH

A basic postulate underlying the Christian curriculum is that "all truth is God's truth."[10] From the biblical viewpoint, God is the Creator of everything. Therefore, truth in all fields stems from Him. Failing to see this point clearly has led many to construct a false dichotomy between the secular and the religious. That dichotomy implies that the religious has to do with God, while the secular is divorced from Him. From that point of view, the study of science, history and mathematics is seen as basically secular, while the study of religion, church history, and ethics is viewed as religious.

That is not the biblical perspective. In the Scriptures, God is seen as the Creator of the objects and patterns of science and math, as well as the Director of historical events. In essence, there are no secular aspects of the curriculum. John Henry Newman pointed to that truth when he wrote that "it is easy enough" on the level of thought "to divide Knowledge into human and divine, secular and religious, and to lay down that we will address ourselves to the one without interfering with the other; but it is impossible in fact."[11]

All truth in the Christian curriculum, whether it deals with nature, humanity, society, or the arts, must be seen in proper relationship to Jesus Christ as Creator and Redeemer. It is true that some forms of truth are not addressed in the Scriptures. For example, nuclear physics is not explained in the Bible. That, however, does not mean that nuclear physics is not connected with God's natural laws or that it does not have moral and ethical implications as its applications affect the lives of people. Christ was the Creator of all things—not just those things people have chosen to call religious (John 1:1–3; Col. 1:16).

All truth, if it be truth indeed, is God's truth, no matter where it is found. As a result, the curriculum of the Christian school must be seen as a unified whole, rather than as a fragmented and rather loosely connected assortment of topics. Once that viewpoint is recognized, education will have taken a major step forward in creating an atmosphere in which the "Christian mind" can develop—an educational context in which young people can be taught to think "Christianly" about every aspect of reality.[12]

THE STRATEGIC ROLE OF THE BIBLE IN THE CURRICULUM

A second postulate follows that of the unity of all truth: The Bible is the foundational and contextual document for all curricular items in the Christian school. This postulate is a natural outcome of a bibliocentric, revelational epistemology. Just as special revelation forms the basis of epistemological authority, so also it must be the foundation of the curriculum. Our discussion of epistemology noted that the Bible is not an exhaustive source of truth. Much truth exists outside of the Bible, but it is important to note that no truth exists outside the metaphysical framework of the Bible. "The teaching authority of Scripture," Arthur Holmes asserts, "commits the believer at certain focal points and so provides an *interpretive framework*, an overall glimpse of how everything relates to God."[13]

The concept of an interpretive framework needs constant emphasis in Adventist education. The Bible is not the whole of knowledge, but it does provide a frame of reference within which to study and interpret all topics. Whether that framework is the view of evolutionary naturalism, the Greek and Roman classics, the biblical worldview, or some other perspective makes a great deal of difference. An Adventist school is Christian only when it teaches all subjects from the perspective of God's Word.

Elton Trueblood noted that "the important question is not, Do you offer a course in religion? Such a course might be offered by any institution. The relevant question is, Does your religious profession make a difference? . . . A mere department of religion may be relatively insignificant. The teaching of the Bible is good, but it is only a beginning. What is far more important is the penetration of the central Christian convictions into the teaching" of every subject.[14]

Frank Gaebelein was making the same point when he wrote that there exists "a vast difference between education in which devotional exercises and the study of Scripture have a place, and education in which the Christianity of the Bible is the matrix of the whole program or, to change the figure, the bed in which the river of teaching and learning flows."[15]

An educational system that maintains a split between the areas it defines as secular or religious can justify tacking on religious elements to a basically secular curriculum. It may even go so far as to treat the Bible as the first among equals in terms of importance. But the school whose constituency and teachers embrace the idea that all truth is God's truth will find itself bound by that belief to develop a curricular model in which the biblical worldview permeates every aspect of the curriculum.

According to Ellen White, "the science of redemption is the science of all sciences," and the Bible is "the Book of books."[16] Only an understanding of that "science" and that "Book" makes everything else meaningful in the fullest sense. Viewed in the light of "the grand central thought" of the Bible, Ellen White points out, "every topic has a new significance."[17] Every student, she noted in another connection, should gain a knowledge of the Bible's "grand central theme, of God's original purpose for the world, of the rise of the great controversy, and of the work of redemption. He should understand the nature of the two principles that are contending for supremacy, and should learn to trace their working through the records of history and prophecy, to the great consummation. He should see how this controversy enters into every phase of human experience; how in every act of life he himself reveals the one or the other of the two antagonistic motives; and how, whether he will or not, he is even now deciding upon which side of the controversy he will be found."[18]

The conflict between good and evil has left no area of existence untouched. On the negative side, we see the controversy in the deterioration of the world of nature, in war and suffering in the realm of history and the social sciences, and in the concern with lostness in the humanities. On the positive side, we discover the wonder of a natural order that seems to be purposefully organized, humanity's ability to relate to and care for others in social life, and the deep visions and desires of individuals for wholeness and meaningfulness. "Why," every individual is forced to ask, "is there evil in a world that seems so good? Why is there death and sorrow in an existence that is so delicately engineered for life?"

The questions go on and on, but without supernatural aid, earthbound humans are helpless as they seek to discover ultimate answers. They can discover bits and pieces of "truth" and build theories concerning their meaning, but only in God's cosmic breakthrough to humanity in its smallness and lostness is that ultimate meaning provided.

God's special revelation contains the answers to humankind's big questions. It is that revelation, therefore, that must provide both the foundation and the context for every human study. Each topic within the curriculum, and even human life itself, takes on new meaning in the light of God's Word. It is imperative, therefore, that Adventist schools teach every subject from the biblical perspective.

Gaebelein, in his classic treatment of the issue, has suggested that what we need is the "integration" of every aspect of the school program with the biblical worldview. Integration "means 'the bringing together of parts into the whole'"[19] "The call, then," he writes, "is for a wholly Christian worldview on the part of our education. We must recognize, for example, that we need teachers who see their subjects, whether scientific, historical, mathematical, literary, or artistic, as included within the pattern of God's truth."[20] That is the rightful place of religion in education, claimed Henry P. Van Dusen in his Rockwell Lectures, not because the churches say so or because it is dictated by tradition, but *because of the nature of Reality.*"[21] After all, God is the being whose existence brings unity and meaning to the universe, and it is His revelation that provides unity and meaning to the curriculum.

Unfortunately, in the most common curriculum design, Bible or religion is just one topic among many, as illustrated in Figure 3. In that model, every topic is studied in the context of its own logic, and each is regarded as basically independent of the others. History or literature teachers are not concerned with religion, and religion teachers do not involve themselves with history or literature, since all teach their own

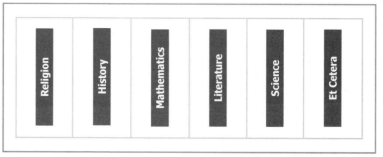

FIGURE 3.   Curriculum Model: Self-Contained Subject Matter Areas

specialty. Each subject has its own well-defined territory and tradi-tional approach. This model rarely delves into the relationship between fields of study, let alone their ultimate meaning.

In an attempt to correct the above problem, some enthusiastic reformers have gone to the other extreme and developed a model that is illustrated in Figure 4. This model seeks to make the Bible and reli-gion into the whole curriculum, and, as a result, also misses the mark, since the Bible never claims to be an exhaustive source of truth. It sets the framework for the study of history and science and touches upon those topics, but it is not a textbook for all areas that students need to understand. On the other hand, it *is* a textbook in the science of salva-tion and a source of inspired information concerning both the order-liness and the abnormality of our present world, even though it never claims to be a sufficient authority in all areas of possible truth.

A third organizational scheme could be labeled the foundational and contextual model (see Figure 5). It implies that the Bible (and its

FIGURE 4.   Curriculum Model: The Bible as the Whole

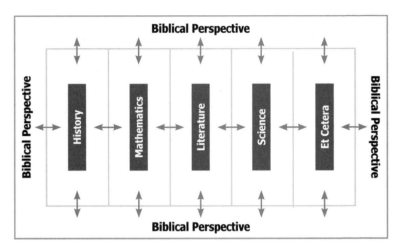

FIGURE 5.   Curriculum Model: The Bible as Foundational and Contextual

worldview) provides a foundation and a context for all human knowledge, and that its overall meaning infuses every area of the curriculum and adds significance to each topic. This corresponds with what Richard Edlin helpfully refers to as the "*permeative* function of the Bible." "The Bible," he notes, "is not frosting on an otherwise unaltered humanist cake. It needs to be the leaven in the educational loaf, shaping the entire curriculum from its base up as it permeates through the whole school program."[22] Figure 5 sets forth an integration model, indicating that educators in Adventist schools must approach each subject in the light of the biblical perspective in order to understand its fullest meaning.

The broken lines in Figure 5 signify the lack of rigid divisions between the various subjects, and the absence of any false dichotomy between the sacred and the secular. The two-headed arrows indicate not only that the Bible helps us understand every topic in the curriculum, but also that the study of history, science, and so on also sheds light on the meaning of Scripture. God has revealed Himself through the Bible in a special revelation and through His created world in a general revelation. We can grasp the full significance of the latter only in the light of the former, but both shed light on each other since all truth has its origin in God. Every topic in the curriculum has an impact upon every other, and all achieve maximum meaning when integrated within the biblical context.

CHRISTIANITY AND THE RADICAL REORIENTATION OF THE CURRICULUM

One of the challenges that educators must face in developing a biblically oriented curriculum in the twenty-first century is the diverse worldviews that permeate contemporary society, including that of postmodernism, which claims that there is no such thing as a genuine worldview anchored in reality—that all worldviews or grand narratives are human constructions. But that claim is itself a worldview with definite metaphysical and epistemological presuppositions.[23]

That thought raises the issue of the general lack of self-consciousness evidenced by most people. Harry Lee Poe reflects upon that topic when he writes that "every discipline of the academy makes enormous assumptions and goes about its business with untested and unchallenged presuppositions. We are used to this. Assumptions and presuppositions have become so much a part of the fabric of life that we do not notice the threads. These threads make up the worldview of the culture in which we live. They are the things 'everybody knows' and that, therefore, go untested. They are so deeply ingrained in us that we are rarely even aware of them."[24] In short, worldviews for many people are subliminal—a part of the larger culture that is accepted without challenge.

On the other hand, Poe notes that "in the marketplace of ideas, the fundamental assumptions . . . to which people cling are the very things that Christ challenges."[25] Clearly, the biblical worldview and the predominant mentality of the larger culture are often at odds, and there are different religious and even different Christian worldviews. Making people aware of the contrasts results in what sociologist Peter Berger refers to as "collisions of consciousness"[26] and what philosopher David Naugle labels "worldview warfare."[27]

From that perspective, by its very nature, the biblically based curriculum challenges other methods of curricula organization and suggests a radical reorientation of the subject matter in Adventist schools. The essential point that the Adventist educator must grasp is that *the teaching of any topic in an Adventist school must not be a modification of the approach used in non-Christian schools. It is rather a radical reorientation of that topic within the philosophical framework of Christianity.*

A good place to begin examining the radical reorientation of the curriculum is the field of literary study.[28] The study of literature holds a crucial position in all school systems because literature addresses and seeks to answer people's most important questions; reveals humanity's basic desires, wishes, and frustrations; and develops insight into human experience. Beyond raising aesthetic sensitivity, the study of literature leads to inductive insights in such areas as psychology, philosophy, religion, history, and sociology; and it provides information about such topics as human nature, sin, and the meaning and purpose of human existence.

The impact of literary study is all the more powerful because it is delivered in a package with which humans emotionally identify. That is, it reaches people at the affective and cognitive levels simultaneously. In the fullest sense of the words, literary content is philosophical and religious because it deals with philosophical and religious issues, problems, and answers. Literary study, therefore, holds a central position in curricular structures and provides one of the most powerful educational tools for the teaching of religious values.

Secularist John Steinbeck caught the significance of the central core of great literature in his classic *East of Eden:* "I believe that there is one story in the world, and only one. . . . Humans are caught—in their lives, in their thoughts, in their hungers and ambitions, in their avarice and cruelty, and in their kindness and generosity too—in a net of good and evil. . . . There is no other story."[29]

While there may be no other story, there are certainly multiple interpretations of the implications of that story. For Steinbeck, from his earthbound perspective, there is no hope. The end is always disastrous despite hopeful signs along the way. By way of contrast, the Bible features hope in spite of serious problems. It also explores the "only story," but with revelatory insight into the meaning of a world that forms the battleground for a cosmic clash between the forces of good and evil.

The responsibility of the literature teacher in the Adventist school is to help students learn to read critically so that they can grasp the meaning of their assignments in terms of the great controversy between good and evil.[30] Literary study is not merely a relaxing excursion into the realm of art. T. S. Eliot observed that what we read affects "the whole of what we are. . . . Though we may read literature merely for pleasure, of 'entertainment' or of 'aesthetic enjoyment,' this reading never affects simply a sort of special sense: it affects our moral and religious existence."[31] There is no such thing as artistic neutrality. The function of literary study in an Adventist school is not just to help students become learned in the great writers of the past and present; it must also help them to view with more clarity and sensitivity the issues at stake in the controversy between good and evil.

The Bible in this context provides an interpretive framework that transcends human insights. "Every topic," including literature, "has a new significance," Ellen White suggests, when viewed in the light of the "grand central theme" of the Scriptures.[32] The Bible is quite a realistic book. Those literary extremes that ignore evil at one end of the spectrum or glorify it at the other are neither true nor honest and certainly allow no room for a viable concept of justice. The challenge for Christians is to approach literary study in such a way that it leads readers to see the reality of humanity and its world as it actually is— filled with sin and suffering, but not beyond hope and the redeeming grace of a caring God.

The interpretive function of literary instruction has generally been approached in two different ways (see Drawings A and B in Figure 6). Drawing A represents a classroom approach that emphasizes the literary qualities of the material and uses the Bible or ideas from the Bible

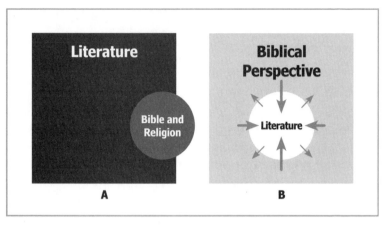

FIGURE 6.   The Contextual Role of the Biblical Perspective

from time to time as asides. The only difference between this approach and the way literature is taught in non-Christian institutions is that biblical insights are added.

Drawing B depicts the study of literature in the context of the biblical perspective and its implications for humanity's universal and personal dilemmas. It interprets literature from the distinctive vantage point of Christianity, recognizing both the abnormality of the present world and God's activity in that world. Using that approach, the study of literature in a Christian institution can be richer than in a secular school, since non-Christians are handicapped by their lack of the all-important (in terms of insight and interpretation) biblical view of sin and salvation. That does not mean that literary elements such as plot and style are unimportant, but rather that they are not, within the context of Christianity, the most important aspects of literary study.

Note also that in Drawing B the arrows indicate a two-way transaction between the biblical perspective and literary study. Not only does the biblical worldview help us interpret literature, but literary insights also help us to better understand religious experience within the context of religious truth.

Adventist teachers must help students move beyond the story to the meaning of its insights for daily life. The function of literary study in a Christian institution, Virginia Grabill writes, is to help students learn how to "think" about the issues of life—their personal identity and purpose, the presence of good and evil, justice and forgiveness, the beautiful and the ugly, sexuality and spirituality, ambition and humility, joy and suffering, purity and guilt, and so on.[33]

C. S. Lewis made a similar point when he wrote that "one of the minor rewards of conversion is to be able at last to see the real point of all the literature we were brought up to read with the point left out."[34] The goal of literary study in a Christian school is not to transmit a body of knowledge, but to develop a skill—the ability to think critically and to interpret literary insights from the perspective of the biblical worldview.

We have spent a great deal of time examining literary study in the reoriented Christian curriculum. Similar observations could be made about history and social studies. History in the Christian curriculum is viewed in the light of the biblical message as God seeks to work out His purpose in human affairs. The Bible is seen as providing the interpretive framework for events between the fall of Adam and the second coming of Jesus. The Bible is not treated as a comprehensive history textbook, but as an account that focuses on the history of salvation. There are, of course, points of intersection between general history and the Bible in terms of events, prophecy, and archaeology. But the Christian teacher of history realizes that the specific points of intersection are in the minority, and that the major function of the Bible in his or her discipline is to provide a perspective for understanding.

The same might be said of the life, physical, and social sciences, or physical education, or agriculture in the curriculum of an Adventist school. The Bible provides the framework for understanding a troubled world, while the disciplines bring forth the bits and pieces. The Bible provides the pattern that gives interpretative meaning to the otherwise meaningless details uncovered by the scholar. The Bible thus becomes the focal point of integration for all of human knowledge.

That fact is especially important in the sciences, an area in which the past century has witnessed one of the most significant cultural wars of all time. Unfortunately, unproven hypotheses related to macroevolution[35] have too often been granted the status of fact and then been used to provide the interpretive framework for science in most schools.

The basic problem: The cosmologies of macroevolution and biblical creationism are incompatible. The latter begins with a perfect creation, continues on with humanity's fall into sin, and then transitions to God's solution for removing the effects of the Fall. But the macroevolution scenario is diametrically opposed to the biblical model. From the perspective of macroevolution, all creatures originated as less complex organisms and have been improving through the processes of natural selection. In that model there is no need for redemption and restoration.

The biblical framework for interpreting natural history is constructed from the Genesis account, which states that God created the earth in six days, and that He created human beings in His own image. The basic facts of the Genesis creation story do not allow for either macroevolution (in which God has no involvement) or theistic evolution (which limits God to the role of mere initiator of the evolutionary process). Adventist schools must be unapologetically creationist. The biblical metaphysic stands at the very foundation of why the Seventh-day Adventist Church chose to establish Adventism's educational alternative.

The integration of human knowledge into the biblical framework is important, but it must be done with care and wisdom. Frank Gaebelein, in discussing how to develop correlations between Christian concepts and the subject matter of the various fields of study, points out some necessary cautions. A major pitfall, as he sees it, is the danger "of a false integration through forced correlations that are not truly indigenous to the subject in question. Such lugging in of stilted correlations, even though motivated by Christian zeal, is liable to do more harm than good through giving the impression that integration of specific subjects with God's truth is a put-up job.

"What may be needed is a more relaxed attack upon the problem and a clearer realization of the limits under which we are working.

Here a suggestion by Emil Brunner is useful. Speaking of the distortion brought into our thinking through sin, he sees it at its greatest in such areas as theology, philosophy, and literature, because these are nearest man's relation to God and have thus been most radically altered through the fall. They therefore stand most in need of correction, and in them correlation with Christianity is at its highest. But as we move from the humanities to the sciences and mathematics, the disturbance through sin diminishes almost to the vanishing point. Thus the Christian teacher of the more objective subjects, mathematics in particular, ought not to seek for the detailed and systematic correlations that his colleagues in psychology, literature, or history might validly make."[36]

Gaebelein does not mean that there are no points of contact between Christianity and topics such as mathematics, but rather that they are fewer and less obvious.[37] Christian teachers will utilize those points while not seeking to force integration in an unnatural manner.

However, the integration of mathematics and the physical sciences with Christian belief may be even more important than the integration of literature and the social sciences with Christianity because many students have imbibed the idea that they are objective, neutral, and functional and have no philosophical presuppositions, biases about reality, or cosmological implications. On the contrary, the study of mathematics and the hard sciences is totally embedded in bias and assumption.

Mathematics, for example, like Christianity, is built upon unprovable postulates. Beyond that, assumptions such as the orderliness of the universe and the validity of empirical observation are metaphysical and epistemological presuppositions that undergird science but are rejected by many modern and postmodern people in both Western and Eastern cultures. It is essential to make these assumptions evident in class presentations because they are often taken as facts and are invisible to the average student who has been raised in an age that has placed its uncritical faith in science and mathematics rather than in the Creator of scientific and mathematical reality. This integration is most natural at the elementary, secondary, and introductory college levels, since courses at theses levels provide the intellectual context for such sophisticated courses as theoretical mechanics and advanced calculus.

Christian math and science teachers will also creatively utilize the natural points of integration between their subject matter and religion. Mathematics, for example, certainly has contact points with the Christian faith when it deals with such areas as infinity and the existence of numbers in other parts of daily life, from music to crystallography and astronomy. The world of mathematical precision is God's world; thus, mathematics is not outside the pattern of God's truth.[38]

Before moving away from the radical reorientation of the curriculum, we need to emphasize that it is of the utmost importance for Adventist educators and their constituents to realize that *the biblical worldview must dominate the curriculum of our schools to ensure that they are Adventist in actuality rather than merely in name.* Adventist educators must ask themselves this probing question: If I, as a teacher in an Adventist school, am teaching the same material in the same way that it is presented in a public institution, then what right do I have to take the hard-earned money of my constituents? The answer is both obvious and frightening. Adventist education that does not provide a biblical understanding of the arts, sciences, humanities, and the world of work is not Christian. One major aim of Adventist education must be to help students think Christianly.

THE BALANCED CURRICULUM

Beyond the realm of specific subject matter in the Adventist school is the larger issue of the integration of the curricular program in such a way that it provides for the balanced development of the various attributes of students as they are being restored to their original position as beings created in the image and likeness of God. In the section on the nature of the student, we noted that at the Fall humanity, to a large extent, experienced a fracturing of that image in the spiritual, social, mental, and physical realms. We also saw that education is basically an agent of redemption and restoration as God seeks to use human educators to restore fallen individuals to their original state. The curriculum must, therefore, establish an integrated balance that facilitates that restoration. It cannot focus merely on mental development or career preparation. It must develop the whole person—the physical, social, spiritual, and vocational as well as the mental needs of each student.

Unfortunately, traditional education focused almost exclusively on the mental. Greek idealism set the stage for more than two millennia of miseducation that ignored or denigrated both physical development and preparation for useful vocations.

By contrast, the Bible is neither anti-physical nor anti-vocational. After all, God created a physical earth He deemed "very good" (Gen. 1:31), and He intends to resurrect human beings with physical bodies at the end of time (Phil. 3:21; 1 Thess. 4:13–18). Beyond that, Jesus was educated to be a carpenter, and the wealthy Paul was trained as a tent maker even though it appeared that he would never need to work at the trade.

But those biblical principles were obscured in the early centuries of the Christian Church when its theology amalgamated with Greek thought. That resulted in some very non-biblical educational theory and practice.

The nineteenth century experienced a wave of reform, with calls for a return to balanced education. Ellen White spoke about that needed reform. In fact, it was at the center of her educational philosophy. We saw that in the very first paragraph of *Education*, in which she noted that "true education . . . is the harmonious development of the physical, the mental, and the spiritual powers."[39]

To restore individuals to wholeness, Adventist education cannot neglect the balance between the physical and the mental. The importance of that balance is highlighted by the fact that it is the body that houses the brain, which people must use in order to make responsible spiritual decisions. Whatever affects one part of a person affects the total being. Individuals are wholistic units, and the curriculum of the Adventist school must meet all their needs to ensure that they achieve wholeness and operate at peak efficiency. Ellen White was speaking about the traditional imbalance in education when she wrote that "in the eager effort to secure intellectual culture, physical as well as moral training has been neglected. Many youth come forth from institutions of learning with morals debased, and physical powers enfeebled; with no knowledge of practical life, and little strength to perform its duties."[40] The practical aspects of life were important to Ellen White's sense of educational balance. Thus she could write that "for their own physical health and moral good, children should be taught to work, even if there is no necessity so far as want is concerned."[41]

Balance is equally important in the informal or extracurricular aspects of the school's curriculum. This includes a multiplicity of organizations and activities, such as clubs, musical groups, athletics, work experiences, school publications, and so on, which must all be brought into harmony with the purpose of the institution and integrated with the Christian message, just as is the formal curriculum, to ensure that the school does not give a dichotomous message to its students, constituency, and onlookers. The Adventist school has two major tasks in regard to the informal curriculum—the choice of activities and the creation of guidelines for the implementation of the activities selected. Both of those tasks must be based on biblical values.

That thought brings us to the topic of values education throughout the curriculum. Arthur Holmes made an important point when he noted that "education has to do with the transmission of values."[42] The issue of values is central to much of the conflict over education today. What we find in most places, including schools, is an ethical relativism that goes against the very core of the Bible's teachings. When modern culture lost the concept of an eternal God it also lost the idea that there are universal values that apply across time, individuals, and cultures. Ronald Nash was correct when he asserted that "America's educational crisis is not exclusively a crisis of the mind," but also a crisis of the "heart," a values crisis.[43] This crisis is evident not only in schools, but also in the public media, which all too often promotes values that are non-Christian or even anti-Christian.

These are realities that the Adventist school cannot afford to ignore. The good news is that Christian educators, operating within the biblical framework, have a strategic advantage over those with other orientations because they have an epistemological and metaphysical grounding for their value system, which is not available to others. As Robert Pazmiño puts it, "the Christian educator can propose higher values because he or she can answer such questions as: What are persons and their ultimate end? What is the meaning and purpose of human activity? What, or rather, who is God? These questions can be answered with a certainty and surety which is not possible outside of a revealed faith."[44]

Pazmiño also points out the existence of a hierarchy of values, with spiritual values providing the context for evaluating options in ethics and aesthetics, as well as in the scientific, political, and social realms.[45] That being the case, Christian educators must purposefully develop formal and informal curricula in the light of biblical values. The biblical value system stands at the very foundation of Christian education.

And, we need to note, the values taught in a biblically based school system will not relate only to individual decision-making but will also reflect upon the social whole. Like the Old Testament prophets, Adventist education will raise significant issues related to social justice in an unjust world because biblical valuing involves the public as well as the private world of believers.

As we view the Christian curriculum in all of its complexity, we must never forget the controversy between the forces of good and the powers of evil within our metaphysics, epistemology, axiology, and our individual lives. The conflict between Christ and Satan is evident in the curriculum. Each Adventist school is a battlefield in which the forces of Christ are being challenged by the legions of Satan. The outcome will, to a large extent, be determined by the position given to the Bible in the Adventist school. If Adventist schools are to be truly

Christian, then the biblical perspective must be the foundation and context of all that is done.

POINTS TO PONDER

- Discuss why the Bible is so important in Christian education.
- In what ways does Herbert Spencer's question ("What Knowledge Is of Most Worth?") help us understand a Christian curriculum?
- What are the curricular implications of truth being unified?
- What do we mean when we say that the Bible is the foundation and context of a Christian approach to curriculum?
- Why must the curriculum in a Christian school be radically reoriented? What are the classroom implications of that reorientation?
- What do Adventist educators mean when they speak of a balanced curriculum?

Notes

1. Daryl Eldridge, "Curriculum," in *Evangelical Dictionary of Christian Education*, ed. Michael J. Anthony (Grand Rapids, MI: Baker, 2001), 188.
2. Les L. Steele, *On the Way: A Practical Theology of Christian Formation* (Grand Rapids, MI: Baker, 1990), 186.
3. Herbert Spencer, *Education: Intellectual, Moral, and Physical* (New York: D. Appleton, 1909), 1–87; see especially, pages 10 and 11.
4. Ibid., 13–14.
5. Ibid., 63, 84–86.
6. Mark Van Doren, *Liberal Education* (Boston: Beacon Press, 1959), 108.
7. Alfred North Whitehead, *The Aims of Education and Other Essays* (New York: Free Press, 1967), 7.
8. C. P. Snow, *The Two Cultures: And a Second Look* (New York: Cambridge University Press, 1964).
9. Gaebelein, "Toward a Philosophy of Christian Education," 41.
10. Holmes, *All Truth Is God's Truth.*
11. John Henry Newman, *The Idea of a University* (Notre Dame, IN: University of Notre Dame Press, 1982), 19. On the false dichotomy between the sacred and the secular, see George R. Knight, *Myths in Adventism: An Interpretive Study of Ellen White, Education, and Related Issues* (Hagerstown, MD:

Review and Herald, 2009), 127–138.

12. Harry Blamires, *The Christian Mind* (London, S.P.C.K., 1963); Holmes, *All Truth Is God's Truth*, 125.

13. Arthur F. Holmes, *The Idea of a Christian College*, rev. ed. (Grand Rapids, MI: Eerdmans, 1987), 18; emphasis added.

14. Trueblood, "The Marks of a Christian College," 163.

15. Gaebelein, "Toward a Philosophy of Christian Education," 37.

16. White, *Education*, 126; White, *Counsels to Parents, Teachers, and Students*, 442.

17. White, *Education*, 125.

18. Ibid., 190.

19. Gaebelein, *The Pattern of God's Truth*, 7.

20. Ibid., 23.

21. Henry P. Van Dusen, *God in Education* (New York: Charles Scribner's Sons, 1951), 82.

22. Richard J. Edlin, *The Cause of Christian Education* (Northport, AL: Vision Press, 1994), 63–66.

23. See Harry Lee Poe, *Christianity in the Academy: Teaching at the Intersection of Faith and Learning* (Grand Rapids, MI: Baker, 2004), 22–23.

24. Ibid.

25. Ibid., 22.

26. Quoted in Naugle, *Worldview: The History of a Concept*, xvii.

27. Ibid.

28. For a fuller treatment of the topic of literature in the Adventist curriculum, see Knight, *Myths in Adventism*, 153–174; Knight, *Philosophy and Education: An Introduction in Christian Perspective*, 4th ed., 229–233.

29. John Steinbeck, *East of Eden* (New York: Bantam, 1955), 355.

30. A helpful aid to reading in Christian perspective is James W. Sire, *How to Read Slowly: A Christian Guide to Reading with the Mind* (Downers Grove, IL: InterVarsity, 1978).

31. T. S. Eliot, "Religion and Literature," in *The Christian Imagination: Essays in Literature and the Arts*, ed. Leland Ryken (Grand Rapids, MI: Baker, 1981), 148–150.

32. White, *Education*, 125, 190.

33. Virginia Lowell Grabill, "English Literature," in *Christ and the Modern Mind*, ed. Robert W. Smith (Downers Grove, IL: InterVarsity, 1972), 21.

34. Quoted in Frank E. Gaebelein, *The Christian, the Arts, and Truth: Regaining the Vision of Greatness* (Portland, OR: Multnomah Press, 1985), 91–92.

35. *Macroevolution* is defined as "large scale change in organisms resulting in new species, genera, families, etc." (http://carm.org/evolution-terminology,

accessed May 10, 2012) occurring over long time periods.

36. Gaebelein, "Toward a Philosophy of Christian Education," 47–48.

37. For Gaebelein's discussion of the integration of Christianity and mathematics, see *The Pattern of God's Truth*, 57–64.

38. For one of the more sophisticated treatments of the practical aspects of the integration of the sciences, mathematics, and other fields with Christianity, see Harold Heie and David L. Wolfe, eds., *The Reality of Christian Learning: Strategies for Faith-Discipline Integration* (Grand Rapids, MI: Eerdmans, 1987).

39. White, *Education*, 13. See also Ellen G. White, *Christ's Object Lessons* (Washington DC: Review and Herald, 1941), 330; White, *Fundamentals of Christian Education*, 15, 42.

40. White, *Fundamentals of Christian Education*, 71; cf. 21.

41. Ibid., 36.

42. Holmes, *Shaping Character*, vii.

43. Ronald H. Nash, *The Closing of the American Heart: What's Really Wrong with America's Schools* ([Dallas]: Probe Books, 1990), 29–30.

44. Robert W. Pazmiño, *Foundational Issues in Christian Education: An Introduction in Evangelical Perspective*, 2nd ed. (Grand Rapids, MI: Baker, 1997), 99.

45. Ibid., 101.

CHAPTER 6

Methodological Considerations

A major determinant of the teaching and learning methodologies of any philosophy of education consists of the educational goals of that perspective and the epistemological-metaphysical framework in which those goals are couched. The aims of Adventist education go beyond accumulating cognitive knowledge, gaining self-awareness, and coping successfully with the environment. To be sure, Adventist education shares those aspects of learning with other systems of education, but beyond that, it has the more far-reaching goals of reconciling individuals to God and one another and restoring the image of God in them. The methodologies chosen by the Adventist educator must take those preeminent purposes into consideration.

That does not mean that somehow Adventist education will invent unique and original ways of teaching in the same sense that Christianity is a unique religion and Christ is a unique person. Obviously, Adventist educators will use many, if not all, of the same methods as other teachers. They will, however, select and emphasize those methodologies that best aid them in helping their students to develop Christlike characters and reach the other goals of Adventist education.

EDUCATION, THINKING, SELF-CONTROL, AND DISCIPLINE

Central to the issue of the development of Christian character is recognizing that human beings are not simply highly developed animals that respond to reward and punishment. The Bible pictures human beings as being created in the image of God and having, even in their fallen state, the ability to think reflectively.

Because humans can engage in reflective thought, they can make meaningful decisions about their own actions and destiny. Students in an Adventist school must be educated to think for themselves rather than merely be trained, like animals, to respond to environmental cues. Human beings, created in God's image, are to be educated "to be thinkers, and not mere reflectors of other men's thought."[1] It is true that there are some training aspects in the human learning process, but those approaches generally dominate only when the person is very young or mentally impaired. The ideal, as we shall see below, is to move as rapidly as possible, with any given student, from the training process to the more reflective educative process.

At the heart of Adventist education is the goal of empowering students to think and act reflectively for themselves rather than just to respond to the word or will of an authority figure. Self-control, rather than externally imposed control, is central in Adventist education and discipline. Ellen White put it nicely when she wrote that "the discipline of a human being who has reached the years of intelligence should differ from the training of a dumb animal. The beast is taught only submission to its master. For the beast, the master is mind, judgment, and will. This method, sometimes employed in the training of children, makes them little more than automatons. Mind, will, conscience, are under the control of another. It is not God's purpose that any mind should be thus dominated. Those who weaken or destroy individuality assume a responsibility that can result only in evil. While under authority, the children may appear like well-drilled soldiers; but when the control ceases, the character will be found to lack strength and steadfastness. Having never learned to govern himself, the youth recognizes no restraint except the requirement of parents or teacher. This removed, he knows not how to use his liberty, and often gives himself up to indulgence that proves his ruin."[2]

It is for that reason that Ellen White never seemed to tire of driving home the point that "the object of discipline is the training of the child for self-government. He should be taught self-reliance and self-control. Therefore as soon as he is capable of understanding, his reason should be enlisted on the side of obedience. Let all dealing with him be such as to show obedience to be just and reasonable. Help him to see that all things are under law, and that disobedience leads, in the end, to disaster and suffering."[3]

Please note that in the above quotations Ellen White ties together education, thinking, self-control, and discipline. That is an important insight and one that we too often overlook. In fact, most people equate discipline with punishment. But they are two quite distinct concepts. Ideally, punishment comes into play only after discipline has failed. Punishment is a negative, remedial activity, whereas discipline is positive and stands at the core of developing a Christian character.

In a Christian approach to education, human beings must be brought to the place where they can make their own decisions and take responsibility for those choices without continually being coaxed, directed, and/or forced by a powerful authority. When that goal is achieved, and the power to think and to act upon one's thoughts is internalized, then people have reached moral maturity. They are not under the control of another, but are making their own moral decisions about how to act toward God and other people. Such is the role of self-control in the shaping of human beings in the image of God. Psychiatrist Erich Fromm makes the same point when he writes that "the mature person has come to the point where he is his own mother and his own father."[4]

Discipline is not something an authority figure does to a child, but something that adults help children learn to do for themselves. John Dewey, America's most influential twentieth-century philosopher, reflected on that point when he wrote that "a person who is trained to consider his actions, to undertake them deliberately . . . is disciplined. Add to this ability a power to endure in an intelligently chosen course in the face of distraction, confusion, and difficulty, and you have the essence of discipline. Discipline means power at command; mastery of the resources available for carrying through the action undertaken. To know what one is to do and to move to do it promptly and by use of the requisite means is to be disciplined."[5]

Discipline as self-control has its roots deep in the Christian concepts of character development, responsibility, and perseverance. We noted earlier that character development is one of the major aims of Adventist education. Character development and discipline are inextricably entwined. "Strength of character," Ellen White wrote, "consists of two things—power of will and power of self-control."[6] The will, furthermore, "is the governing power in the nature of man, the power of decision, or choice."[7] Part of the function of Christian discipline in the home and school is to guide and mold the power of the will as students move toward maturity.

Internal discipline concentrates on developing children's wills through allowing them to make choices and to experience the consequences. Arthur Combs has pointed out that "responsibility is learned from *being given* responsibility; it is never learned from having it withheld. . . . Learning to be responsible requires being allowed to make decisions, to observe results, and to deal with the consequences of those decisions. A curriculum designed to teach responsibility needs to provide continuous opportunities for students to engage in such processes. To do so, however, requires taking risks, a terribly frightening prospect for many teachers and administrators."[8]

But even the very problem of allowing others to make mistakes arises from the nature of God and His love. After all, He created a universe in which mistakes are possible when He could have established one that was fool-proof—but only at the price of creating humans as something less than beings in His image. Beings without genuine choices are automatons rather than free moral agents. God created humans in such a way as to make character development a definite possibility. It is important to remember that when people do not have the option of making wrong choices, neither do they have the ability to make correct ones. People cannot develop character if they are constantly controlled through having their choices curtailed. They are then, in essence, merely complex machines rather than moral agents created in God's image. Love and freedom are risky and dangerous, but they are the way God has chosen to run His universe.

In a Christian framework, the answer to a lack of discipline is not bigger and better strategies to bring young people under control, but conscious development and application of techniques to build self-control and a sense of responsibility in each child. We gain nothing if by authoritative methodologies we manage to produce quiet, order, and student conformity while sacrificing intelligent behavior, responsibility, and creativity.

Developing intelligent self-control in others is not an easy task. Ellen White writes that "this work is the nicest [most delicate and discerning], the most difficult, ever committed to human beings. It requires the most delicate tact, the finest susceptibility, a knowledge of human nature, and a heaven-born faith and patience."[9]

The number of biblically based books written on this crucial aspect of Adventist education is not great. The best place to begin is the chapter entitled "Discipline" in Ellen White's *Education*.[10] It is perhaps the most insightful chapter that she ever wrote in the field of education. Deeply rooted in a Christian philosophy, it is a methodological exposition second to none. Reading those eleven pages every week for his or her entire career would enrich every teacher's ministry. Here are a few samples from that chapter:

- "The wise educator, in dealing with his pupils, will seek to encourage confidence and to strengthen the sense of honor. Children and youth are benefited by being trusted. . . . Suspicion demoralizes, producing the very evils it seeks to prevent. . . . An atmosphere of unsympathetic criticism is fatal to effort."[11]
- "The true object of reproof is gained only when the wrong-doer himself is led to see his fault and his will is enlisted for

its correction. When this is accomplished, point him to the source of pardon and power."[12]

- "Many youth who are thought incorrigible are not at heart so hard as they appear. Many who are regarded as hopeless may be reclaimed by wise discipline. These are often the ones who most readily melt under kindness. Let the teacher gain the confidence of the tempted one, and by recognizing and developing the good in his character, he can, in many cases, correct the evil without calling attention to it."[13]

Such are the challenges and possibilities of redemptive discipline in line with Christ's ministry of seeking the lost and shaping the characters of those in a relationship to God through Him. Many of the principles of redemptive discipline are expounded upon in a very practical way in Jim Roy's *Soul Shapers*,[14] which describes the methodologies that lie at the foundation of the practice of Adventist education.

One model that describes the progressive internalization of discipline appears in Figure 7. It illustrates in a general way the relationship between internal and external control and the weaning process that is the goal of redemptive discipline. Infants and extremely young children need a great deal of external control, but the maturation process should lead progressively to greater self-control and less external control, until individual children have reached the point of moral maturity. At that time, they are ready to take their place as responsible persons in the adult world. Christian discipline, therefore, is both a positive and a liberating power. It "is not," A. S. De Jong points out, "to keep the child down or to break him, but to lift him up or to heal him; for that reason discipline may be called upon to repress only in order to set free, to train children in the exercise of the freedom of the children of God."[15] The end product of Christian discipline will be young people who "do right because they believe it is right and not because some authority tells them to."[16]

The connection between the developing of self-control and the restoration of the image of God has serious implications for educators as they select appropriate methodologies for the Christian school.

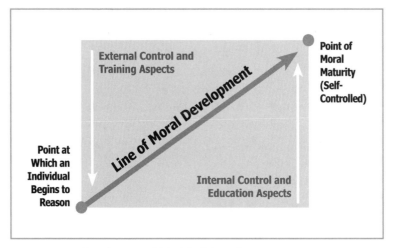

FIGURE 7.   A Developmental Model of Discipline

That concept should act as a screening device for Adventist educators as they choose learning and teaching strategies for the classroom. They must utilize those methodologies that will help to develop what Harro Van Brummelen refers to as "*responsible* disciples."[17]

BEYOND COGNITION TO COMMITMENT AND RESPONSIBLE ACTION

Closely related to the above discussion is the idea that Christian knowing is not merely passive. It is, as we noted in our discussion of epistemology, an active, dynamic experience. Thus, in a Christian school, instructional methodology must move beyond strategies for passing on information. Nicholas Wolterstorff forcefully argues that Christian education "must aim at producing alterations in what students tend (are disposed, are inclined) to do. It must aim at tendency learning." He points out that Christian schools must move beyond techniques for merely teaching the knowledge and abilities required for acting responsibly, since students can assimilate those ideas without developing a "tendency to engage in such action." Thus "a

program of Christian education will take that further step of culti-
vating the appropriate *tendencies* in the child. It will have tendency
learning as one of its fundamental goals."[18]

Donald Oppewal has developed a teaching methodology explic-
itly based upon the dynamic epistemology of Scripture. While noting
that actual practice is the ideal, Oppewal suggests a three-stage
instructional methodology aimed to produce a dynamic learning
experience. In the *consider* stage, the learner is presented with the
new material. During the second phase—the *choose* phase—"the
options for response are clarified and their implications better understood. . . . If the first phase dramatizes what it *is* the learner faces, the
second phase highlights whatever *oughts* are involved." In the third
stage—the *commit* phase—students move "beyond intellectual
understanding, beyond exposure of the moral and other considerations and toward commitment to act on both the is and the ought."
Commitment to a form of action, claims Oppewal, is the very mini-
mum expectation in the context of biblical knowing and teaching.[19]
A fourth stage, of course, needs to be added whenever possible and
practicable; namely the *action* phase. In that phase opportunity for
acting on those commitments is provided.

THE BIBLE AND INSTRUCTIONAL METHODOLOGY

The central epistemological source for Christians, the Bible, provides a
wealth of information related to methodologies used by God in the process of educating human beings. Even a casual reading of the Old Testament reveals that ancient Israel was immersed in a total educational
environment, which was consciously constructed to aid in the spiritual,
intellectual, social, and physical development of its citizens. That environment was structured to provide lifelong learning experiences
through holidays, sabbatical years, historic memorials, the arts, home
instruction, public reading of the Torah, and a host of other devices.

The Bible makes it plain that this educational environment was to
be used to awaken inquiry and develop curiosity in the minds of the

young. The interest thus developed was to be followed by deliberate instruction. Note, for example, the instructions given for the highly symbolic keeping of the Passover. Moses wrote that observing this ritual would lead the young to ask, "What do you mean by this service?" and that the family elders would then have a natural opportunity to engage the minds of the youth in a meaningful learning experience (Exod. 12:25–27; see also 13:3–16; Deut. 6:20–25). A major principle underlying Old Testament pedagogy is that instruction should not be forced upon unready minds. Rather, instructional methods used in the Old Testament capitalized upon human beings' natural interest in a topic in order to engage the people's minds in a dynamic interchange. Central to the whole educational complex of ancient Israel was the sacrificial system, which pointed forward to the life, death, and work of Jesus. That system, with its pageantry, beauty, and life-taking awesomeness, provided one of the major object lessons of the ancient world. It was an educational device that taught through both its appeal to the senses and the curiosity it generated.

Moving into the New Testament, we find Jesus as the ultimate teaching model. "In the Teacher sent from God," Ellen White asserts, "all true educational work finds its center."[20] We can learn a great deal about appropriate methods for conveying the Christian message, both in schools and elsewhere, through an examination of the specific teaching techniques Christ used and the way He related to people. We examined the relationship aspect of His teaching above in the chapter on the ministry of teaching. Here our focus will be on His instructional methods. This short discussion is at best an introduction to that topic. But the Christian educator can glean a great deal about the subject through an inductive and analytical study of Christ's methods in the Gospels. Ellen White's education-related books are also very insightful on the topic.[21]

Roy Zuck has noted that "Jesus succeeded as a masterful Teacher" largely because of "his remarkable ability to capture the interest of his audience." He aroused "their desire to learn what he was teaching."[22]

That was especially true in His use of parables, object lessons, and provocative questions.

Perhaps the most obvious teaching method of Jesus was His use of illustrations. Two of His most frequent illustrative formats were the parable and the object lesson. Parables form a large portion of Jesus's teachings recorded in the New Testament—about 25 percent of Mark and 50 percent of Luke is in the form of parables. The parable has the advantages of being concrete, appealing to the imagination, and having intrinsic interest. John Price has written that "people who turn away from facts and arguments will listen readily to stories. Not only that, but they will remember them and be influenced by them."[23]

Part of the power of Christ's parables comes from their relevance to the everyday lives of His hearers. When He dealt with the lost sheep, the sowing of seeds, and the good Samaritan, He was describing things in people's daily experience. That aroused interest, engaged their minds, and helped them remember the story and its lesson as they interacted with the topics of His parables in their daily living.

A second method of illustration used by Jesus was the object lesson. While standing on a hillside, He discusses the topic of anxiety. Reaching down to pluck a lily, He notes its beauty, and gives the lesson that if God so clothed "the grass of the field, which today is alive and tomorrow is thrown into the oven, will he not much more clothe you" (Matt. 6:30). His use of the coin in His discussion about the paying of taxes certainly made His accompanying words more effective (Matt. 22:15–22).

Commenting on Christ's teaching methods, Ellen White wrote that "in parables and comparisons He found the best method of communicating divine truth. In simple language, using figures and illustrations drawn from the natural world, He opened spiritual truth to His hearers, and gave expression to precious principles that would have passed from their minds, and left scarcely a trace, had He not connected His words with stirring scenes of life, experience, or nature. In this way He called forth their interest, aroused inquiry, and when He had fully secured their attention, He decidedly impressed upon

them the testimony of truth. In this way He was able to make sufficient impression upon the heart so that afterward His hearers could
look upon the thing with which He connected His lesson, and recall
the words of the divine Teacher."[24]

Another of Jesus's teaching methods was the use of thought-com-
pelling questions. He used the 213 separate questions recorded in the
Gospels to drive home spiritual truths, to draw out responses of commitment, and to deal with His detractors. Regarding that last point,
teachers at times have students who would like to put them on the
spot. Jesus answered His detractors' questions by asking questions. By
using that strategy, He could maneuver them into answering their
own questions. His success in the disciplinary use of questions is
attested to by the fact that after a series of questions engineered to
trap Him "no one dared to ask Him any question" (Mark 12:34).

In regard to the use of questions as a learning device, John A.
Marquis has written that "teaching is not telling, because a great deal
of our telling elicits no mental response. So our Lord had a habit of
throwing in a question now and then that broke up the serenity of his
class and made them sit up and think."[25] The aim of the Christian
teacher is not to control minds, but to develop them.

Jesus's pedagogical methodology utilized both theory and practice. For example, He alternated periods of instruction devoted to the
disciples with times when He sent them out to apply what they had
learned (Matt. 10:5–15; Luke 10:1–20). That undoubtedly helped them
realize their need for further instruction, fixed the successful lessons in
their minds, and kept them from separating the theoretical from the
experiential. The practical side of education is a most effective teach-
ing-learning device. Jesus was more interested in conveying knowledge
that would help men and women in their daily lives than He was in
presenting knowledge as an abstraction. In the process, He united theoretical knowledge with both daily life and the eternal realities of the
kingdom of God and the great controversy between good and evil.

So much more can be said about the teaching methods of Jesus,
but will have to be left to your future study. Meanwhile, we will close

with three insightful quotes from Ellen White. First, "Christ always used simple language," yet His words had depth of meaning and spoke to the heart.[26] Second, "in His teaching He came down to" the level of His students.[27] And, third, "Jesus did not disdain to repeat old, familiar truths," yet "He separated [them] from the companionship of error," and "reset them in their proper framework."[28] That last statement is the informative, integrative, and interpretive function of Christ's teaching methodology—a function, we noted in our study of the Christian curriculum, which must stand at the center of all Adventist education.

POINTS TO PONDER

- Why is it that a Christian teaching methodology will not be unique?
- Discuss the educational implications of the relationship of thinking, self-control, and discipline.
- What is the relationship between discipline and punishment?
- In what ways can teachers help move students from cognition to responsible action?
- What are the main methodological lessons that we can learn from the teaching ministry of Jesus?

Notes

1. White, *Education*, 17.
2. Ibid., 288.
3. Ibid., 287.
4. Erich Fromm, *The Art of Loving* (New York: Harper and Brothers, 1956), 44.
5. John Dewey, *Democracy and Education* (New York: Free Press, 1966), 129.
6. White, *Counsels to Parents, Teachers, and Students*, 222.
7. White, *Education*, 289.
8. Combs, *Myths in Education,* 139–140.
9. White, *Education*, 292.
10. Ibid., 287–297.
11. Ibid., 289–291.
12. Ibid., 291.

13. Ibid., 294.

14. Roy, *Soul Shapers.*

15. A. S. De Jong, "The Discipline of the Christian School," in *Fundamentals in Christian Education*, ed. Cornelius Jaarsma (Grand Rapids, MI: Eerdmans, 1953), 397.

16. Dudley, *Why Teenagers Reject Religion and What to Do About It*, 89.

17. Harro Van Brummelen, *Walking with God in the Classroom* (Burlington, Ontario: Welch Publishing, 1988), 34.

18. Nicholas Wolterstorff, *Educating for Responsible Action* (Grand Rapids, MI: Eerdmans, 1980), 15, 14.

19. Donald Oppewal, *Biblical Knowing and Teaching,* Calvin College Monograph Series (Grand Rapids, MI: Calvin College, 1985), 13–17.

20. White, *Education*, 83.

21. See, e. g., White, *Counsels to Parents, Teachers, and Students*, 259–263; White, *Fundamentals of Christian Education*, 47–49; 236–241; White, *Education*, 73–83.

22. Roy B. Zuck, *Teaching as Jesus Taught* (Grand Rapids, MI: Baker, 1995), 158. See also Zuck's *Teaching as Paul Taught* (Grand Rapids, MI: Baker, 1998).

23. J. M. Price, *Jesus the Teacher* (Nashville: The Sunday School Board of the Southern Baptist Convention, 1946), 101.

24. White, *Fundamentals of Christian Education*, 236.

25. John A. Marquis, *Learning to Teach from the Master Teacher* (Philadelphia: Westminster, 1916), 29.

26. White, *Counsels to Parents, Teachers, and Students*, 261.

27. Ibid., 180.

28. White, *Fundamentals of Christian Education*, 237.

CHAPTER 7

The Social Function of Adventist Education

Before delving into the specifics of Adventist education's social function, we need to consider the cultural transmission function of education. We find that function in the Bible. Abraham was chosen because God saw that he would be faithful in teaching his household (Gen. 18:19), God through Moses gave the Israelites an educational system that touched every phase of their lives, and Jesus's parting words were "teach all nations" (Matt. 28:19, 20, KJV).

THE STRATEGIC ROLE OF EDUCATION

Education holds a strategic position in every society because all youth must pass through some type of educational experience to prepare them to fill society's responsible positions. The future of any society will be shaped by its current youth. And the direction they will take that society will to a large extent be determined by their education. Thus the control of educational institutions and the content to be taught in those institutions has been a perennial social issue.

George S. Counts has noted that "to shape educational policy is to guard the path that leads from the present to the future. . . . Throughout the centuries since special educational agencies were first established, the strategic position of the school has been appreciated by kings, emperors, and popes, by rebels, reformers, and prophets. Hence, among those opposing forces found in all complex societies, a struggle for the control of the school is always evident. Every group or sect endeavors to pass on to its own children and to the children of others that culture which it happens to esteem; and every privileged class seeks to perpetuate its favored position in society by means of education."[1]

Likewise, Counts has observed, the failure of revolutions has been a record of their inability to bring education into the service of the revolutionary cause. Revolutionary bodies will possess no more permanence than the small bands of idealists who conceived them if the children of the next generation cannot be persuaded to embrace the values of the revolution. Therefore, the history of both the Soviets and the National Socialists has demonstrated that one of the first measures taken by revolutionary governments is to place all educational agencies under the direct control of the state and to give the schools a central part in building the new society.[2]

A similar logic, of course, stimulated the formation of the American and other democratic educational systems. And in that logic we find the genesis of the Adventist interest in education in all its forms. Ellen White picked up on that thinking when she wrote that "with such an army of workers as our youth, rightly trained, . . . how soon the message of a crucified, risen, and soon-coming Saviour might be carried to the whole world! How soon might the end come—the end of suffering and sorrow and sin! How soon, in place of a possession here, with its blight of sin and pain, our children might receive their inheritance where 'the righteous shall inherit the land, and dwell therein forever.'"[3]

ADVENTIST EDUCATION'S CONSERVATIVE AND REVOLUTIONARY ROLES

God's ideal for Seventh-day Adventist education reflects both a conservative social function and a revolutionary one. It is to be conservative in the sense that it seeks to transmit the unchanging truths of the Bible across time, but it is to be revolutionary as a change agent of a righteous God in a sinful world.

In that latter posture, it seeks to change the *status quo* on the individual level through the conversion of human beings from their old way of life to the Christian way. *Transformation, conversion,* and *death and rebirth* are some of the words that the Bible applies to the dynamics of Christianity as it transforms the lives of individuals, moving them from an orientation of self-centeredness to one of God-centered service to both Him and other people.

But change at the individual level is only one aspect of the church's revolutionary role. It is also to be an agent for broader change in the ongoing struggle for social justice in a sinful world. It is part of God's ideal not only to feed the poor (Matt. 25:31–46), but also to help make this earth a better place to live through social reform.

But once again, the revolutionary role must not stop there. According to the Bible, social reform, for all of its good points, is insufficient to straighten out a crooked world driven by the forces of sin and human greed. The only real solution to the sin problem as pictured in the Bible is the Second Advent. While the Gospels set forth that truth (see Matt. 24), it is especially evident in the Book of Revelation. That book in particular indicates the divine solution to earth's woes. Thus the apex of the church's revolutionary function is not merely to transform people from sinful selfishness to a life of service or to organize them to become change agents for earthly reform, but to preach a message that helps prepare the world for the end of history and the establishment of a new earth built upon God's principles. That new earth, the Bible tells us, does not come about through human effort, but as the result of God's breaking into human history through Christ's second coming. That event is the Event of events in world history. It is the ultimate revolution.

Seventh-day Adventism from its beginning has viewed itself as an agent of God in that ultimate revolution. In particular, it has seen its calling to be the preaching of the apocalyptic message of the three angels that stands at the heart of the Book of Revelation (Rev. 14:6–12); a message that God commanded to be given immediately before the Second Advent (vv. 14–20). It is a worldwide message that calls people back to faithfulness to God, even as human societies move toward their final end. It is a message of the coming Christ who will not only feed the poor but abolish hunger; who will not only comfort the grieving but eradicate death (Rev. 21:1–4). Adventism has been called to preach to a lost world the ultimate Hope that by comparison pales all other hopes. The central purpose of Adventism is to preach that ultimate Hope. And the principal reason for the establishment of Adventist schools is to prepare people for that event and for the task of spreading the good news of the coming Savior.

Within that revolutionary apocalyptic context, the conservative function of Adventist education is twofold: (1) to pass on the legacy of Bible truth, and (2) to provide a protected atmosphere in which that transmission can take place and in which Christian values can be imparted to the young in their formative years through both the formal curriculum and the informal aspects of the educational program, such as the peer group and extracurricular activities.

The Christian Church and its adherents have the unique role of being in the world, without being of the world (John 17:14–18). How to achieve that seemingly contradictory position has remained a challenge to the church since the time of Christ.

The separatist strand of the paradox has led the church to establish protected atmospheres for its youth during their formative years, such as religious schools and youth groups. Such agencies act as refuges where young people from Adventist families can learn skills, attitudes, values, and knowledge without being overwhelmed by the worldview and cultural mores of the larger society. The atmosphere in which these activities take place is designed to be conducive to the transferring of Adventist culture to the younger generation. Parents and church members are willing to support this type of education financially because they recognize that it differs philosophically from the cultural milieu of the larger society, and they believe that the Adventist worldview is the correct one in terms of metaphysics, epistemology, and axiology.

Seen from such a viewpoint, the primary function of the Adventist school is not to be an evangelistic agency to convert unbelievers (even though that may be a side result), but rather to help young people from Adventist homes meet Jesus and surrender their lives to Him. Implicit in this function is a distinct realization that if the majority of the student peer group in a denominational school does not espouse Adventist values, then the school's spiritual mission probably will not be accomplished. Adventist education's conservative function therefore provides a protected atmosphere for the nurturing of the church's youth; an environment in which all values, skills, and aspects of knowledge can be taught from the Adventist philosophic perspective.

Beyond the conservative function of Adventist education is its revolutionary role. At the beginning of the Christian era, Christ's great gospel commission sent His disciples into all the world to make disciples of all nations, and to teach people everything that He had commanded (Matt. 28:19, 20). And at the end of the Christian era Christ has commanded that the good news of salvation, Second Advent, and coming judgment also be preached "to every nation and tribe and tongue and people" (Rev. 14:6). While the commission of Matthew 28 has been sounded by Christianity at large, the Church has neglected the imperative of Revelation 14. It is that latter commission that forms the basis for the existence of Seventh-day Adventism. From its inception, the church has believed that it has a unique commission to preach the three angels' messages of Revelation 14:6–12 to all the earth before the Second Advent (vv. 14–20). Adventism's message is a call to faithfulness to God as earthly history moves toward its final days. The evangelistic imperative of Revelation 14 has literally driven Adventism to every part of the earth.

Christian churches (including Seventh-day Adventism) have too often been conservative bastions of society, when they should function as agents for change. The life of Jesus as portrayed in the Bible can best be seen as modeling change rather than conservatism. He was the Reformer of reformers. And He called out a people to become change agents in His ongoing mission.

The conservative functions of a Christian school are important because they play a role in the church's revolutionary task of preparing its youth to become evangelistic workers. That does not mean, it should be emphasized, that all students will be educated for church employment. Each one will, however, be trained to be a witness to the love of God in a sinful world, regardless of his or her career goals.

As such, the Adventist school can be seen as a staging ground for Christian activism and missionary work. It provides, ideally, not only the knowledge underlying the evangelistic imperative of the church, but also practical, guided activities in the larger community that ensure that students develop the skills necessary to meet people with the message of Jesus and to perform their individual roles in the context of God's church on earth. Edward Sutherland wrote that in God's plan "the Christian school should be the nursery in which reformers are born and reared—reformers who would go forth from the school burning with practical zeal and enthusiasm to take their places as leaders in these reforms."[4]

In summary, the social function of the Adventist school has both a conservative and a revolutionary aspect. The comingling of those two roles empowers the developing student to be in the world but not of the world. In essence, the function of the Adventist school is to educate the youth of the church for service to God and their neighbors, rather than to train them for self-service through the acquisition of a "good job" and a comfortable income. Those outcomes, of course, may be by-products of Adventist education, but they are not central to its purpose.

Service to others was the essence of Christ's life, and it is therefore the ultimate aim of Adventist education. In harmony with the Bible, Adventist education will develop Christians who can relate well to others in this world. But even more important, Adventist schools will educate students for citizenship in the kingdom of heaven.

POINTS TO PONDER

- Discuss the strategic role of education. In what ways is the control of education central to the flow of civilization?
- What is the conservative function of Adventist education?
- What is the revolutionary role of Adventist education?
- Which is more important—the conservative or the revolutionary role? Why?

Notes

1. Chapman and Counts, *Principles of Education,* 601, 602.

2. See George S. Counts, *The Soviet Challenge to America* (New York: John Day, 1931), 66–67.

3. White, *Education*, 271.

4. E. A. Sutherland, *Studies in Christian Education: Educational Experiences Before the Midnight Cry Compared with Educational Experiences Before the Loud Cry* (Leominster, MA: Eusey Press, [1952]), 72.

CHAPTER 8

Closing Perspective

The education that does not furnish knowledge as enduring as eternity, is of no purpose."[1] That frank statement was not made by a narrow religious bigot, but by a person who in the same paragraph writes that "it is right that you should feel that you must climb to the highest round of the educational ladder. Philosophy and history are important studies; but your sacrifice of time and money will avail nothing, if you do not use your attainments for the honor of God and the good of humanity. Unless the knowledge of science is a stepping-stone to the attainment of the highest purposes, it is worthless. . . . Unless you keep heaven and the future, immortal life before you, your attainments are of no permanent value. But if Jesus is your teacher, not simply on one day of the week, but every day, every hour, you may have His smile upon you in the pursuit of literary acquirements."[2] For Ellen White, the value of education was related to perspective. A broad literary education was of great value *if* it kept eternal realities, goals, and values at the forefront.

That perspective brings us to the ultimate questions regarding Adventist education that must be asked by parents, school boards, Adventist educational professionals, and the church at large: Why support Seventh-day Adventist schools? Why should the church spend hundreds of millions of dollars each year to support thousands of schools around the world when free, high-quality public education is often available? How can the denomination justify such expenditures in the light of the other pressing needs of the church and the world it serves? The answer to such questions obviously has a link to the purpose of Adventist education. If Adventist schools fulfill a sufficiently distinctive and important purpose, the achievement of that purpose is worth the expense.

That answer brings us to the frontier of why there should be Christian (rather than specifically Adventist) schools in general. We have noted throughout the study of the topic that Christian education is the only education that can meet people's deepest needs, because only Christian educators understand the core of the human problem. The redemptive aim of Christian education is what makes it Christian. The primary function of Christian education is to lead young people into a transforming, saving relationship with Jesus Christ. It is in the context of that relationship that such secondary functions as academic achievement, character development, the formation of a Christian mind, and education for social responsibility and the world of work must of necessity take place. But it is crucial to realize that all but one of those secondary goals can take place in a non-Christian school. Thus, when Christian educators aim only at the goals that fall within the realm of all education, they have failed even before they begin. As a result, *when Christian educators neglect to emphasize the redemptive role of their schools, they make their schools both unimportant and unnecessary.*

But what about distinctively Adventist Christian schools? What justifies their existence if all Christian schools ideally aim at the redemptive function of education? The answer to those questions brings us to the heart of why the Seventh-day Adventist Church even exists as a separate Christian denomination.

Too often, we see Adventism as merely another denomination with a few different doctrines and some countercultural dietary practices. But the core of Adventist identity from its very inception has been its conviction that it is a movement of prophecy, a church with a special message to proclaim to all the world as set forth in the heart of the Apocalypse of John.[3] And there are sound biblical reasons for that understanding. Revelation 12:17 highlights the fact that at the end of time God will have a people who keep all His commandments and that their commandment keeping will eventually stimulate a reaction from the last-day dragon power. "And the dragon," John wrote, "was wroth with the woman, and went to make war with the remnant of her seed, which keep the commandments of God" (KJV). Revelation 13 and 14 pick up that theme, with chapter 13 expanding on the dynamics of the last-day dragon power, and chapter 14 presenting the message of the last-day woman (church), climaxing with the second advent of Christ. In that context, the three angels' messages of Revelation 14:6–12 highlight an everlasting gospel that is to be preached to all the world, a judgment-hour emphasis as earth's history moves toward its conclusion, a call to worship the Creator God in contrast to honoring the beast, and a declaration regarding the fall of oppressive Babylon that has confused humanity by substituting human words for the word of God. The third angel climaxes its message in verse 12, which reads: "Here is the patience of the saints: here are they that keep the commandments of God, and the faith of Jesus" (KJV).

Seventh-day Adventists noted from their beginning that the Sabbath commandment is emphasized in Revelation 12–14. At the end of time, we are told in Revelation 14, everybody will be worshipping somebody: either the Creator God of the Sabbath who made heaven and earth and sea (14:7; Gen. 2:1–3; Exod. 20:8–11) or the beast (Rev. 14:9). And Adventists have been quick to note that immediately after the giving of the three angels' messages Christ comes to harvest the earth (vv. 14–20).

While the general Christian community has largely ignored those messages in their eschatological context, Seventh-day Adventism found in them its marching orders and purpose as a distinct denomination. It is that purpose that has literally driven Adventism to the ends of the earth until it has become the most widespread unified Protestant body in the history of Christianity. Adventists have been willing to sacrifice their lives and their money to achieve that goal. And in the process they have developed a church organization to spearhead that thrust and an educational system and publishing ministry to enlighten and convict its membership and prepare them to either go to all the world themselves or to sponsor others to fulfill the denomination's unique mission. It is no accident that Adventism sent its first overseas missionary and opened its first denominationally sponsored school the same year (1874). Nor is it coincidental that every major revival in Adventist education has been stimulated by a revival in its apocalyptic mission.[4]

We dare not become bashful about that mission. It is the only valid reason for the existence of Seventh-day Adventism. The possibility of losing its apocalyptic vision and Adventism's place in prophetic history is the greatest threat that the denomination and its educational system face.[5]

That threat brings me to my next point. *An Adventist educational ministry that has lost its hold on the apocalyptic vision has failed—not just partially, but totally.*

Let me illustrate the depth of the problem. Some time ago, I received a call from an academy principal who had been inspired by my keynote at the 2006 North American Division educational convention on "Seventh-day Adventist Education and the Apocalyptic Vision."[6] As a result, he determined to hire teachers who truly understood the uniqueness of Adventism and its mission to the world. With that commitment in mind, he went to the local Adventist college and interviewed each of the graduating education majors. His question to each was the same: "What is the difference between Adventist education and evangelical Christian education?" Not one student could tell him. Somehow, he concluded, that college had failed in passing on Adventism's unique identity and mission, even though the institution had been established to develop educational professionals.

That thought brings me to the bottom line—*Adventist education is important only if it is truly Adventist.* A school that has lost sight of its reason for being, that has forgotten its message and mission, will eventually lose its support. And it should. To be absolutely frank, *a Seventh-day Adventist school that is not both Christian and Adventist is an unnecessary institution.* All its functions can be achieved by schools in the evangelical sector, and most of them by the public sector.

Pastor Shane Anderson is right on target in his recently published *How to Kill Adventist Education* when he points out that "Adventist parents increasingly aren't willing to pay the price to send their kids" to institutions that have lost their purpose. *"After all,"* he writes, *"why pay thousands of dollars to send your child to a school that is now no longer substantially different from the average Christian school—or the local public school—down the street?"*[7]

With that insight, we are back to the importance of the study of the philosophy of education and *Knight's Law* and its two corollaries. Put simply, *Knight's Law* reads that "It is impossible to arrive at your destination unless you know where you are going." Corollary Number 1 declares: "A school that does not come close to attaining its goals will eventually lose its support." Corollary Number 2 states: "We think only when it hurts." The purpose of the study of Adventist educational philosophy is to get those who teach and administer in Adventist schools thinking before it hurts and to put them in a proactive mode to develop schools that are educative in the fullest sense, while at the same time being both self-consciously Christian and Adventist.

POINTS TO PONDER

- What is the essential contribution of all Christian schools to education?
- What is the unique Adventist contribution to Christian education?
- In what ways can Adventist education totally fail in its mission?
- In looking back over this book, discuss the ways that the study of the philosophy of biblical/Christian/Adventist education can help you shape your ideas and practice.

Notes

1. White, *Fundamentals of Christian Education*, 192.

2. Ibid.

3. See George R. Knight, *A Search for Identity: The Development of Seventh-day Adventist Beliefs* (Hagerstown, MD: Review and Herald, 2000); George R. Knight, *The Apocalyptic Vision and the Neutering of Adventism*, rev. ed. (Hagerstown, MD: Review and Herald, 2009).

4. See George R. Knight, "The Dynamics of Educational Expansion: A Lesson from Adventist History," *The Journal of Adventist Education* 52, no. 4 (April/May 1990): 13–19, 44–45.

5. See Knight, *Apocalyptic Vision*, for an extended treatment of that threat.

6. George R. Knight, "Adventist Education and the Apocalyptic Vision," *The Journal of Adventist Education* 69, no. 4 (April/May 2007): 4–10; 69, no. 5 (Summer 2007): 4–9.

7. Anderson, *How to Kill Adventist Education*, 22, 56; cf. 30.

BIBLIOGRAPHY

Anderson, Shane. *How to Kill Adventist Education (and How to Give It a Fighting Chance!)*. Hagerstown, MD: Review and Herald, 2009.

Blamires, Harry. *The Christian Mind*. London: S.P.C.K., 1963.

Bruce, F. F. *The Epistle to the Ephesians*. Westwood, NJ: Fleming H. Revell, 1961.

Chapman, J. Crosby, and George S. Counts. *Principles of Education*. Boston: Houghton Mifflin, 1924.

Clark, Gordon H. *A Christian Philosophy of Education*. Grand Rapids, MI: Eerdmans, 1946.

Coleman, James S., et al. *Equality of Educational Opportunity*. Washington, DC: U.S. Department of Health, Education, and Welfare, 1966.

Combs, Arthur W. *Myths in Education: Beliefs That Hinder Progress and Their Alternatives*. Boston: Allyn and Bacon, 1979.

Counts, George S. *The Soviet Challenge to America*. New York: John Day, 1931.

De Jong, A. S. "The Discipline of the Christian School." In *Fundamentals in Christian Education,* ed. Cornelius Jaarsma. Grand Rapids, MI: Eerdmans, 1953.

Dewey, John. *Democracy and Education*. New York: Free Press, 1966.

Ditmanson, Harold H., Harold V. Hong, and Warren A. Quanback, eds. *Christian Faith and the Liberal Arts*. Minneapolis: Augsburg, 1960.

Dudley, Roger L. *Why Teenagers Reject Religion and What to Do About It*. Washington, DC: Review and Herald, 1978.

Eavey, C. B. "Aims and Objectives of Christian Education." In *An Introduction to Evangelical Christian Education*. J. Edward Hakes, ed. Chicago: Moody, 1964.

Edlin, Richard J. *The Cause of Christian Education*. Northport, AL: Vision Press, 1994.

Edwards, Jonathan. "Sinners in the Hands of an Angry God." In *Jonathan*

Edwards, rev. ed. Ed. Clarence H. Faust and Thomas H. Johnson. New York: Hill and Wang, 1962.

Eldridge, Daryl. "Curriculum." In *Evangelical Dictionary of Christian Education*, ed. Michael J. Anthony. Grand Rapids, MI: Baker, 2001.

Eliot, T. S. "Religion and Literature." In *The Christian Imagination: Essays in Literature and the Arts*, ed. Leland Ryken. Grand Rapids, MI: Baker, 1981.

Fromm, Erich. *The Art of Loving*. New York: Harper and Brothers, 1956.

Gaebelein, Frank E. *The Christian, the Arts, and Truth: Regaining the Vision of Greatness*. Portland, OR: Multnomah Press, 1985.

_____. *The Pattern of God's Truth: Problems of Integration in Christian Education*. Chicago: Moody, 1968.

_____. "Toward a Philosophy of Christian Education." In *An Introduction to Evangelical Christian Education*, ed. J. Edward Hakes. Chicago: Moody, 1964.

Garrick, Gene. "Developing Educational Objectives for the Christian School." In *The Philosophy of Christian School Education*, 2nd ed., ed. Paul A. Kienel. Whittier, CA: Association of Christian Schools International, 1978.

Geisler, Norman L. and William D. Watkins. *Worlds Apart: A Handbook on World Views*, 2nd ed. Grand Rapids, MI: Baker, 1989.

Glasser, William. *Schools without Failure*. New York: Harper and Row, 1975.

Grabill, Virginia Lowell. "English Literature." In *Christ and the Modern Mind*, ed. Robert W. Smith. Downers Grove, IL: InterVarsity, 1972.

Haynes, Carlyle B. *Righteousness in Christ: A Preacher's Personal Experience*. Takoma Park, MD: General Conference Ministerial Association, [c. 1926].

Heie, Harold, and David L. Wolfe, eds. *The Reality of Christian Learning: Strategies for Faith-Discipline Integration*. Grand Rapids, MI: Eerdmans, 1987.

Henry, Carl F. H. *Christian Personal Ethics*. Grand Rapids, MI: Eerdmans, 1957.

Heschel, Abraham J. *Who Is Man?* Stanford, CA: Stanford University Press, 1965.

Hobbes, Thomas. *Leviathan*, ed. Richard E. Flathman and David Johnston. New York: W. W. Norton, 1997.

Holmes, Arthur F. *All Truth Is God's Truth*. Grand Rapids, MI: Eerdmans, 1977.

————. *The Idea of a Christian College*, rev. ed. Grand Rapids, MI: Eerdmans, 1987.

————. *Shaping Character: Moral Education in the Christian College*. Grand Rapids, MI: Eerdmans, 1991.

Hunter, James Davison. *Culture Wars: The Struggle to Define America*. New York: Basic Books, 1991.

Jahsmann, Allan Hart. *What's Lutheran in Education? Explorations into Principles and Practices*. St. Louis: Concordia, 1960.

Knight, George R. *A Search for Identity: The Development of Seventh-day Adventist Beliefs*. Hagerstown, MD: Review and Herald, 2000.

————. "Adventist Education and the Apocalyptic Vision." *The Journal of Adventist Education* 69, no. 4 (April/May 2007): 4–10; 69, no. 5 (Summer 2007): 4–9.

————. *Myths in Adventism: An Interpretive Study of Ellen White, Education, and Related Issues*. Hagerstown, MD: Review and Herald, 1985, 2009.

————. *Philosophy and Education: An Introduction in Christian Perspective*, 4th ed. Berrien Springs, MI: Andrews University Press, 2006.

————. *The Apocalyptic Vision and the Neutering of Adventism*, rev. ed. Hagerstown, MD: Review and Herald, 2009.

————. "The Dynamics of Educational Expansion: A Lesson from Adventist History." *The Journal of Adventist Education* 52, no. 4 (April/May 1990): 13–19, 44, 45.

LaRondelle, Hans K. *Christ Our Salvation: What God Does for Us and in Us*. Mountain View, CA: Pacific Press, 1980.

Lewis, C. S. *Mere Christianity*. New York: Macmillan, 1960.

Luther, Martin. "Sermon on the Duty of Sending Children to School." In *Luther on Education*, by F. V. N. Painter. Philadelphia: Lutheran Publication Society, 1889.

Marquis, John A. *Learning to Teach from the Master Teacher*. Philadelphia: Westminster, 1916.

Morris, Desmond. *The Naked Ape*. New York: Dell, 1967.

Morris, Van Cleve. *Philosophy and the American School*. Boston: Houghton Mifflin, 1961.

Nash, Paul. *Models of Man: Explorations in the Western Educational Tradition*. New York: John Wiley and Sons, 1968.

Nash, Paul, Andreas M. Kazamias, and Henry J. Perkinson. *The Educated Man: Studies in the History of Educational Thought*. New York: John Wiley and Sons, 1965.

Nash, Ronald H. *The Closing of the American Heart: What's Really Wrong with America's Schools*. [Dallas]: Probe Books, 1990.

Naugle, David K. *Worldview: The History of a Concept*. Grand Rapids, MI: Eerdmans, 2002.

Newman, John Henry. *The Idea of a University*. Notre Dame, IN: University of Notre Dame Press, 1982.

Oppewal, Donald. *Biblical Knowledge and Teaching*. Calvin College Monograph Series. Grand Rapids, MI: Calvin College, 1985.

Pazmiño, Robert W. *Foundational Issues in Christian Education: An Introduction in Evangelical Perspective*, 2nd ed. Grand Rapids, MI: Baker, 1997.

Poe, Harry Lee. *Christianity in the Academy: Teaching at the Intersection of Faith and Learning*. Grand Rapids, MI: Baker, 2004.

Powell, John. *The Secret of Staying in Love*. Niles, IL: Argus Communications, 1974.

Price, J. M. *Jesus the Teacher*. Nashville: The Sunday School Board of the Southern Baptist Convention, 1946.

Pullias, Earl V., and James D. Young. *A Teacher Is Many Things*, 2nd ed. Bloomington, IN: Indiana University Press, 1977.

Ramm, Bernard, *The Pattern of Religious Authority*. Grand Rapids, MI: Eerdmans, 1959.

Rian, Edwin H. "The Need: A World View." In *Toward a Christian Philosophy of Higher Education*, ed. John Paul von Grueningen. Philadelphia: Westminster, 1957.

Rogers, Carl R. *Freedom to Learn*. Columbus, OH: Charles E. Merrill, 1969.

Rookmaaker, H. R. *Modern Art and the Death of a Culture*, 2nd ed. Downers Grove, IL: InterVarsity, 1973.

Roy, Jim. *Soul Shapers: A Better Plan for Parents and Educators*. Hagerstown: MD: Review and Herald, 2005.

Schaeffer, Francis A. *He Is There and He Is Not Silent*. Wheaton, IL: Tyndale House, 1972.

Schumacher, E. F. *A Guide for the Perplexed*. New York: Harper Colophon, 1978.

Sire, James W. *How to Read Slowly: A Christian Guide to Reading with the Mind*. Downers Grove, IL: InterVarsity, 1978.

_____. *The Universe Next Door: A Basic Worldview Catalog*, 5th ed. Downers Grove, IL: InterVarsity, 2009.

Skinner, B. F. *Beyond Freedom and Dignity*. New York: Bantam, 1971.

Snow, C. P. *The Two Cultures: And a Second Look*. New York: Cambridge University Press, 1964.

Spencer, Herbert. *Education: Intellectual, Moral, and Physical*. New York: D. Appleton, 1909.

"Statement of Seventh-day Adventist Educational Philosophy, A." In the *Journal of Research on Christian Education* 10, special edition (Summer 2001): 347–355.

Steele, Les L. *On the Way: A Practical Theology of Christian Formation*. Grand Rapids, MI: Baker, 1990.

Steinbeck, John. *East of Eden*. New York: Bantam, 1955.

Stronks, Gloria Goris, and Doug Blomberg, eds. *A Vision with a Task: Christian Schooling for Responsive Discipleship*. Grand Rapids, MI: Baker, 1993.

Sutherland, E. A. *Studies in Christian Education: Educational Experiences*

Before the Midnight Cry Compared with Educational Experiences Before the Loud Cry. Leominster, MA: Eusey Press, [1952].

Trueblood, David Elton. *A Place to Stand.* New York: Harper and Row, 1969.

———. *General Philosophy.* New York: Harper and Row, 1963.

———. *Philosophy of Religion.* New York: Harper and Row, 1957.

———. *The Idea of a College.* New York: Harper and Brothers, 1959.

———. "The Marks of a Christian College." In *Toward a Christian Philosophy of Higher Education,* ed. John Paul von Grueningen, Philadelphia: Westminster, 1957.

Van Brummelen, Harro. *Walking With God in the Classroom.* Burlington, Ontario: Welch Publishing, 1988.

Van Doren, Mark, *Liberal Education.* Boston: Beacon Press, 1959.

Van Dusen, Henry P. *God in Education.* New York: Charles Scribner's Sons, 1951.

Welch, Herbert. "The Ideals and Aims of the Christian College." In *The Christian College,* by Herbert Welch, Henry Churchill King, and Thomas Nicholson. New York: Methodist Book Concern, 1916.

White, Ellen G. *Christ's Object Lessons.* Washington, DC: Review and Herald, 1941.

———. *Counsels to Parents, Teachers, and Students.* Mountain View, CA: Pacific Press, 1943.

———. *Education.* Mountain View, CA: Pacific Press, 1952.

———. *Fundamentals of Christian Education.* Nashville, TN: Southern Publ. Assn., 1923.

———. *Steps to Christ.* Mountain View, CA: Pacific Press, 1956.

———. *Testimonies for the Church.* 9 vols. Mountain View, CA: Pacific Press, 1948.

Whitehead, Alfred North. *The Aims of Education and Other Essays.* New York: Free Press, 1967.

Wilhoit, Jim. *Christian Education and the Search for Meaning,* 2nd ed. Grand Rapids, MI: Baker, 1991.

Wolterstorff, Nicholas. *Educating for Responsible Action*. Grand Rapids, MI: Eerdmans, 1980.

Zimmerman, Jonathan. *Whose America? Culture Wars in the Public Schools*. Cambridge, MA: Harvard University Press, 2002.

Zuck, Roy B. *Teaching as Jesus Taught*. Grand Rapids, MI: Baker, 1995.

_____. *Teaching as Paul Taught*. Grand Rapids, MI: Baker, 1998.

INDEX